Psychologically Informed Environment Principles in Adult Residential Care

As pressure grows on care managers and staff to work with ever more complex needs, this book is a timely account of how introducing the Psychologically Informed Environment (PIE) principles into a care home will improve work practice and outcomes for residents.

The PIE approach enables staff to:

- Have improved understanding of residents' needs
- Better understand how to respond effectively to complex behaviour
- Introduce trauma-informed practice into their work
- Improve staff support and morale
- Improve outcomes for even the most hard-to-reach clients

Reflecting on one care home's journey to becoming a PIE this book shows how low-cost, high-impact interventions delivered on the frontline can have far-reaching effects on the wellbeing of residents, staff, and the wider culture of the care environment. It will be of interest to all professional, academics, policy-makers, and students working in the fields of adult social services and health and social care more broadly.

Iain Boag has worked in the homeless and residential care sectors since 2001, and is Head of Residential Care Services at St Martins in Norwich. Almost 20 years experience of working on the frontline of homeless and care services has given him invaluable insight into the challenges that homelessness, substance misuse, and poor mental health bring, and of how best to support people with complex needs. Specialising in working with dual diagnosis, Iain is committed to improving outcomes for the most marginalised and hard to reach. Iain lives in Norwich with his wife and two children.

The implementation of the Psychologically Informed Environment (PIE) makes a real difference to some of the most vulnerable and traumatised people in society. This book provides an excellent introduction to the implementation of PIE in an adult residential care setting and gives real examples of how to turn theory into practice.
Dr Jan Sheldon, Chief Executive, St Martins

Psychologically Informed Environment Principles in Adult Residential Care

Iain Boag

LONDON AND NEW YORK

First published 2020
by Routledge
2 Park Square, Milton Park, Abingdon, Oxon OX14 4RN

and by Routledge
52 Vanderbilt Avenue, New York, NY 10017

Routledge is an imprint of the Taylor & Francis Group, an informa business

© 2020 Iain Boag

The right of Iain Boag to be identified as author of this work has been asserted by him in accordance with sections 77 and 78 of the Copyright, Designs and Patents Act 1988.

All rights reserved. No part of this book may be reprinted or reproduced or utilised in any form or by any electronic, mechanical, or other means, now known or hereafter invented, including photocopying and recording, or in any information storage or retrieval system, without permission in writing from the publishers.

Trademark notice: Product or corporate names may be trademarks or registered trademarks, and are used only for identification and explanation without intent to infringe.

British Library Cataloguing-in-Publication Data
A catalogue record for this book is available from the British Library

Library of Congress Cataloging-in-Publication Data
A catalog record for this book has been requested

ISBN: 978-0-367-43647-6 (hbk)
ISBN: 978-1-003-00508-7 (ebk)

Typeset in Times New Roman
by Apex CoVantage, LLC

This book is dedicated to all our residents, past and present, who have let us share their lives.

Contents

	Acknowledgements	viii
	Introduction	1
1	Highwater House	5
2	What is a Psychologically Informed Environment (PIE)?	7
3	Trauma-Informed Care	17
4	Relationships	26
5	Reflective practice	46
6	Elastic tolerance	55
7	Psychological awareness	75
8	Environment	84
9	Evidence	97
10	Rules, roles, and responsiveness (the 3 Rs)	105
11	Staff support and training	114
	Conclusion	126
	Index	130

Acknowledgements

Firstly, I would like to thank the residents of Highwater House who have shared so many stories. I am struck time and again by their resilience in the face of great hardship, and their hope in the face of suffering. It is a pleasure to have worked with so many vibrant, unpredictable and expressive people over the years.

A huge thanks go to Angela and the team at Highwater without whom this book could never have been written. A sentence cannot express the appreciation I feel for the years of support, conversation, argument, and encouragement I have had throughout my career. It is only through their dedication and enthusiasm for their work that the PIE principles have gained such traction in the home. Truly the team represents the best of what it means to care.

Thanks too to Jan and the wider St Martins family for allowing me to draw so heavily from our daily work.

Finally, my greatest thanks go to my family. To my wife, Hannah, whose support, counsel, and straight-talking have guided my life and work for so many years, and whose untiring editing has made this book possible. And to our children, Ella and Tom, thanks for listening to my never-ending musings round the dinner table.

A special mention also goes to Judy, who, when we were chatting about Psychologically Informed Environments, asked – 'Why don't you write a book?'

Introduction

This book introduces the Psychologically Informed Environment (PIE) principles, an innovative framework which care workers can use to improve support and outcomes for residential care service users, particularly those with complex needs.

It is, in principle, an exploration of one residential care home's journey as it becomes a Psychologically Informed Environment. Drawing from trauma-informed practice and using case studies from the home, we will explore the PIE model as a psychosocial intervention which places the service users' experiences and emotions at the heart of the care package; and as a framework that emphasises focus on person-centred care.

At Highwater House, we have found that using the PIE principles has had great effect within the home, impacting positively on staff and resident relationships and the day-to-day running of the service; and it has helped to provide a clear and purposeful narrative for the service. The PIE framework helped us to achieve an overall outstanding rating at our last Care Quality Commission (CQC) inspection. The report says:

> A healthcare professional commented that the staff at Highwater House developed strong, trusting relationships with people using the service. The service promoted a kind, caring and empathetic culture using a new initiative Psychological Informed Environment (PIE) approach. This approach aims to reduce social exclusion and improve the mental health of homeless people. It also aims to improve staff morale and encourage positive interaction. PIE puts the relationships staff develop with people at the very heart of the care process.

The report also highlights some of the statistics which help to prove the model's efficacy, saying:

> Since using the PIE approach, the number of call-outs to the police reduced from 14 in a year to two and untoward incidents reduced from 53 to 20.

The statistics we have gathered over the last three years show a marked decline in the use of emergency services, untoward incidents, and uses of 'time-outs' in the home. Throughout the book you will be introduced, via case studies, to creative approaches we have used when working with challenging residents which have improved outcomes. Using creative behavioural management techniques, or 'elastic tolerance', has helped staff to become increasingly versatile in their work with residents with complex needs.

In 2019 the home won a Homeless Link award for Excellence in Supporting People for its use of the PIE principles; we recently also won the Great British Care Awards regional award for team work. These were unexpected, yet welcome, confirmations of our good work.

Working with a dual diagnosis client group, Highwater House is a relatively unique residential care home. Yet, as pressure grows on the health and social care industry to find creative, cost-effective, ways to work with vulnerable adults, care homes will be expected to accept referrals for increasingly complex individuals, or risk losing funding.

The PIE framework helps frontline workers and managers to meet this challenge, and to find innovative ways to meet their residents' needs.

Throughout this book you are introduced to the PIE principles, and see they are on a continuum of forward-thinking human services – many of the ideas are not new, but refreshed. You are taken through the development of a PIE care home, exploring how the framework can be used on the frontline of social care. The framework is a low-cost, high-impact model – with the key changes to the service being driven by increased staff motivation and understanding of complex needs.

The PIE framework helps to create a strong narrative of person-centred work, an essential ingredient in the running of a successful care home. During inspections the CQC looks for innovative, person-centred and creative approaches to care (mentioned 25, 20, and 16 times respectively throughout the Key Lines of Enquiry (KLOES) prompts and rating characteristics). At the end of each chapter is a reflection of how the topics covered could be assessed using the KLOES (the Key Lines of Enquiry prompts and rating characteristics are available at www.cqc.org.uk/sites/default/files/20171020-adult-social-care-kloes-prompts-and-characteristics-final.pdf, which can be used as a reference guide).

This book is not a step-by-step guide to becoming a PIE, nor is it a research paper. I hope it to be an accessible and informative narrative of how one care home has used the PIE principles to improve its delivery of care.

Being psychologically informed is not a new concept; many elements of the approach should already be embedded in any caring human service. And so, this book has two roles. It will either introduce the reader to the person-centred approach, giving examples of best practice, or it will reinforce and enhance the reader's already good work in this area. Using the PIE principles helps give a strong and positive narrative to a service, promoting residents' strengths and supporting staff to work intuitively and creatively. Care services are asked to find ways to continually improve, and the PIE approach is a framework through which this can happen.

There is no doubt that the care industry is under pressure, and must find ways to respond effectively to changing demands using fewer resources. Having worked at the frontline of a busy care home for almost 20 years, starting as a project worker and now as a manager, I have seen this change first hand, and yet there is, despite austerity biting deeply into social care budgets, hope.

Working with some of the most complex clients living in our community, we have seen the beginning of a sea-change in how care can best be provided, particularly over the last few years amongst progressive human services. The last decade has seen great inroads made into understanding the long-term effects of childhood trauma, with research on brain development in early years supporting what has been known anecdotally on the frontline for years – complex, abusive experiences create in people complex problems, and with them complex behaviours. With this better understanding comes the knowledge that the damage is not a finality – it can be worked with; and so, we have a duty to do so. Clients need not be forever trapped in a spiral of ever worsening health, addiction, and isolation – they can be helped to stabilise and flourish if the environment and support package works *for them*. The wrongs can be righted. The problem is the problem, the person is not the problem. It is increasingly recognised that human connection, and acceptance into a community, is a primary tool in healing trauma. A running theme throughout this book is that people cannot heal in isolation, a connected experience repairs and rebuilds. Providing a supportive, healing environment does not have to cost a lot of money, it only requires thought, consideration and patience, and willingness amongst workers to use themselves as a therapeutic tool as they bear witness to the residents' life stories.

The PIE approach immediately resonated with me as a narrative force which could further this style of biopsychosocial intervention. It chimed with the best aspects of the care we were already providing at Highwater House, and went further still – it gave structure to an elusive 'magic' that comes with working with people with such complex needs for so long. In short, it made sense.

I wanted to write this book because I believe, and have seen, that the PIE formula gives form – a clarity – to a style of work which can help the frontline negotiate the complex world of caring for people with challenging behaviour, addiction, and mental illness. I hope this book will be a welcome addition to the growing number of publications on this subject.

Caveats

Using the PIE principles will enhance workers' approach to their work, and help to create an environment that is supportive for the residents. It does not, however, supplant the need for the excellent governance, audits, safeguarding, or management needed to run a residential care home successfully. In the interests of clarity, throughout this book I presume that the foundations of 'good' care – as inspected by the CQC – are comprehensively in place, and that there is an unwavering compliance to all legislation and legal requirements necessary to run a registered home. Using innovative models of care cannot mean undoing already good practice – they must augment and compliment, build upon, the best of current practice, supporting workers to continually improve.

Throughout the book I have used 'resident', 'client', and 'service user' interchangeably – this is, in part, to recognise that different services use different labels, but also to improve narrative flow.

All of the case studies I have used are based on residents past and present. Their names and histories have been altered to preserve anonymity.

1 Highwater House

Highwater House is a 22-bed residential care home, providing care for men or women aged 18–65 who have a dual diagnosis.

Dual diagnosis is defined as: 'an individual who presents with co-existing mental health (and/or Personality Disorder) and substance misuse problems (drugs and/or alcohol)'.[1] This definition does not begin to express the devastating social and emotional impact that living with such co-morbidity has on people's lives.

In 2005 a dual diagnosis strategy was announced in Norfolk to find ways to improve working with this challenging client group, recognising that 'their behavioural problems and reluctance to engage with services adds to the challenge. Consequently, this group tends to be stigmatised and responsibility passed across agencies.'[2] Highwater House was part of this strategy.

The service is part of St Martins, the Norwich-based homeless charity, which has been supporting vulnerable people since 1972. Consequently, as an organisation, it has adapted many times to the changing needs of the homeless population, and to improved understanding of the causes of homelessness, and has found ways to address these needs with compassion.

I began working for St Martins in 2003, in a service called St Martins House. At that time, it was being recognised that the traditional night shelter could not provide for the complex needs being seen in some of the users. St Martins House was the response to this – a registered premises housing 33 'complex' characters; in it we cared for the homeless who were mentally unwell, and who were struggling to access the night shelter. Some were isolated and unable to cope after the local large mental health hospital closed its doors in the 1990s in favour of providing care in the community, some were too chaotic to use mainstream services – their anti-social behaviour excluding them from much needed support – still others were the product of the failing care system of the 1980s. The home was a sincere attempt to support some of the most troubled and challenging people in the community – people who would become, by and large, to be known as dually diagnosed.

By 2008 St Martins House had undergone a transformation. The building, deemed unfit for purpose, had been renovated, and was renamed Highwater House – reduced to a 22-bed registered care home and with a specific remit to work with dual diagnosis, and so became the service it is today.

The alterations to the building reflected society's changing response to homelessness, mental ill-health, and addiction. The dual diagnosis strategy was a recognition that people were falling through cracks in the system and ending up in chronic isolation, on the streets and unsupported.

The dual diagnosis model we used at Highwater House shifted the focus away from working with homelessness and towards working with vulnerability, and away from coping with our residents' challenges, and towards constructively supporting positive change in them.

This process was not without its difficulties. Workers, skilled in conflict management and used to 'night shelter behaviour', found the increasingly caring role a struggle at times. Introducing new models of support asks staff to change and adapt their own behaviour, which is not always an easy task, or welcome. In the main however the challenge to change was met with a positive, if wary, attitude.

The Psychologically Informed Environment approach has been another such stepping stone on Highwater House's journey, and another leap into the unknown.

The care provided at Highwater House has always mirrored and incorporated changes being enacted across wider society. As part of a relatively small charity it has the ability to be progressive and innovative, being less beholden to statutory mechanisms. With its roots in homelessness it has a 'can do' attitude, a willingness to try new ideas out.

As understanding of how to work with trauma and addiction improves, so the service has reflected this in its care delivery. It is somewhat of a magpie service, and, when prompted by commissioners to find innovative ways to improve the care for its in-need residents, has stretched itself to find new, creative responses.

Highwater House is quite a unique residential care home, and therefore is in the vanguard of pushing the traditional role of a care home beyond its usual boundaries. Some of the characters you will meet within this book may seem extreme as their acute needs are met.

But it is through extremes that we find the centre. I hope that the examples throughout the book help to align that centre in favour of the residents – as individuals in need, and as humans that deserve connection.

Notes

1 Sourced from www.dualdiagnosis.co.uk/uploads/documents/originals/Norfolk%20Dual%20Diagnosis%20Strategy.pdf, 11.
2 Sourced from www.dualdiagnosis.co.uk/uploads/documents/originals/Norfolk%20Dual%20Diagnosis%20Strategy.pdf, 4.

2 What is a Psychologically Informed Environment (PIE)?

In this chapter we will:

- Explore PIE as a psychosocial framework designed to support individuals with complex needs and compound trauma
- Discover that building trusting relationships are key to using the PIE framework
- See PIE to be an adaptable framework suitable for use in all human services
- Be introduced to relationships and reflective practice as the core principles of PIE, and to the five key elements of the PIE model

This chapter introduces the PIE principles as a model of support which places emphasis on building strong, trusting connections between carer and resident; this rapport is used as the key tool to enact change in the resident's life.

Frontline carers are the face of any human service and the gateway through which service users access support; they have more contact – formal and informal – with service users than anyone else; they provide physical care and are often the primary ear; and they provide friendship, guidance, and support throughout the service users' stay at the home.

The importance of this role cannot be overstated. Carers play the role of parent, friend, and advocate; of guardian, nurse, rule-enforcer, and supporter. They are figures of trust and safety as well as of authority. A carer's typical day involves meeting multiple needs in the complex worlds of the residents; the caring role – sometimes official, sometimes benign – is always purposeful. 'There is artistry in human relationships',[1] and carers embody this.

Negotiating this array of roles can be as demanding as it is rewarding, and when working with people with a wealth of mental health and substance use issues, and a lifetime of painful memories, this can be especially so. The innate drive to nurture and to protect, inherent in the carer, can be subsumed by the realities of working with issues of such enormity, of such human catastrophe. Carers need as many tools as possible at their disposal to help them keep their residents, themselves, and fellow workers safe. The PIE framework helps to do so.

Defining a PIE

> Psychologically – 'in a way that affects the mind or relates to the emotional state of a person'
> Informed – 'having or showing knowledge of a subject or situation'
> Environment – 'the surroundings or conditions in which a person, animal, or plant lives or operates'[2]

The many definitions of PIE to be found all agree on a basic tenet: PIE is a humanistic psychosocial model of support which places building relationships between worker and client as the core goal and as the key tool to enact change.

2012 saw the publication of *Psychologically Informed Services for Homeless People – Good Practice Guide* – it is readily available to view and download online, and is a key document in the evolution of the PIE model. In it a PIE is defined as: ' [a service] that takes into account the psychological make-up – the thinking, emotions, personalities and past experience – of its participants in the way that it operates'.[3]

This definition challenges human services to place the client at the heart of their care experience. Despite the *Good Practice Guide* being created to improve support in homeless provisions, the sentiment will resonate throughout any service providing for vulnerable or marginalised people, as residential care homes do.

Inferred in this definition is that services, despite their best intentions, might be primarily answering the needs of the system, staff, or inspectors – with an accidental bias towards the service succeeding rather than the people it is serving. The PIE model, then, aims to redress this systemic bias – another definition of PIE is:

> if asked why the unit is run in such and such a way, the staff would give an answer couched in terms of the emotional and psychological needs of the service users, rather than giving some more logistical or practical rationale, such as convenience, costs, or Health And Safety regulations.[4]

Throughout the book I argue that systems and services created to support vulnerable people can be unintentionally harmful, especially to those who have experienced traumatic events in their lives such as childhood abuse, being sectioned under the Mental Health Act, or who have become socially rootless. The seemingly benign structure of the care home can unwittingly compound previous trauma, notably for those who have spent time in the psychiatric system (as all of our residents at Highwater House have).

However, if workers use the environment mindfully, it is a unique opportunity to enact positive change. The care environment is not passive, nor are carers' actions within it – how workers behave affects the residents either positively or negatively. Using PIE principles can help undo the abrasive damage that constant contact with the care system can inflict on a person. The framework helps workers to put the 'human' before the 'service' in human services.

Another definition of a PIE, provided in *Social Exclusion, Compound Trauma and Recovery*, is: 'a framework for designing "frontline" services that can react as a benign, reflective, complex adaptive system and therefore deal creatively and effectively with complex problems and the complex people experiencing them'.[5]

Working with complex needs can be a frustrating experience. As workers try to support a dual diagnosis client to access other helping services, they can be met with a bewildering set of inclusion criteria – one aspect of the residents' health needs excluding them from accessing help to address another, equally urgent, health-need. At Highwater House our residents have been told time and again: to access counselling you must be sober; to access drug and alcohol services you mustn't be too mentally ill; and to access mental health services you mustn't have a crippling addiction. So, a drug and alcohol service's inclusion criteria might involve a client taking part in group work, but if they suffer from intense social anxiety, born from years of trauma, how will they cope? By self-medicating using alcohol to numb the worst effect of their anxiety. They are then deemed 'not ready to engage' and ejected from the system. Thus, they are placed in a chronic anxiety-making state, the most in need of help unable to access it, caught in a cruel, self-perpetuating cycle.

Our remit at Highwater House has always been to work with such 'unreachable' clients. Historically our primary goal was to provide a safe, albeit containing, space for our residents (reflective of the first stage of trauma recovery).[6] This model of prosthetic care was in many ways a success – helping to keep many highly vulnerable people from the streets – however our residents were living in a static state of chronic addiction and poor mental health. Working with the ensuing behaviours – the conflict, self-harm, and distress – caused by this stasis not only took up a lot of the workers' time but consistently placed them in an authoritative role, and was tiring and sometimes dangerous. Residents played out harmful behaviours time and again as the triggers and causes of their issues were not addressed.

The PIE framework has helped to open new avenues for workers to explore, providing confidence to try new approaches to care. With a renewed focus on not only containing challenging behaviour, but on purposefully adapting their work patterns to reflect best trauma-informed practice, workers are now better able to meet the needs of this complex client group as they move into the next stages of recovery.

Working as a PIE places therapeutic value upon everyday actions around the home. Being acutely aware of our responsibility to work with the whole person and having a framework to understand challenging behaviour has given our staff the freedom to provide a more rounded, and ultimately more rewarding, care package.

Why PIE?

The care home, with 24-hour access to residents, gives a unique opportunity to help individuals disentangle themselves from often multiple diagnoses in a non-clinical setting. The impact of various psychiatric, behavioural, and emotional labels they have been given can be reduced, and workers can support them to create a personal narrative of their choice. This can be a cathartic and de-stigmatising process, with the home's community helping to soothe feelings of distress or dissociation. This is not a new idea – Robert Rapoport's study of therapeutic communities, *Community as Doctor*, surmised that 'living in a community was healing',[7] whilst Herman states 'recovery can only take place within context of relationships'.[8]

We can use our carers' skills – empathy and kindness – to refresh the resident's sense of self who are likely to have spent many years being referred around the mental health system. We can support them to live and tell their story as humans, not clients.

To successfully work in a PIE, we must strive to see the service as our residents do, to mentalise how they might be feeling. Situations which seem routine or unremarkable to the worker might be having a grave effect upon the resident.

Below is a vignette of a section 117 meeting a resident could find themselves in, involving five support services workers:

> *Imagine yourself at home. You have a day off work and have few plans. You make yourself a cup of tea, sit down on your sofa and turn on the TV thinking you'll watch an hour of whatever's on. You relax, comfortable.*
>
> *There's a knock at the door and you're told there's someone here to see you; you can't remember anything having been organised or receiving a letter but you know your memory isn't great, sometimes you don't*

know even what day it is. You take a last sip of tea and go through to another room.

You open the door to a brightly lit room and see there are five people sitting with pens and paper and folders of paperwork sitting at a table watching you as you walk in. You catch the end of a sentence '. . . . there are concerns he will become non-concordant with his medication and stop engaging.'

They introduce themselves in turn – polite, friendly, calm, slowly.

Hi, you'll probably remember me, I'm Jo your Care-Co. I saw you six weeks ago and we talked about how you were feeling. You said you were sometimes feeling in a low mood and I said I'd talk to the psychiatrist and they've organised this meds review. Did you get the letter? How are you feeling today?

Every time you speak different people look down and begin to write notes, then look up and smile at you encouragingly. You feel nervous about what's been written, but even if you were given the notes to look at you can't read well anyway. You can't concentrate and start to feel overwhelmed but don't say anything – they'll only write it down. You don't like being in a room with that many people so you look down and wait for it to be over.

They take it in turns to ask you question after question, kindly but focussed.

Hi, I'm Dr Smith a psychiatrist. Have you had any thoughts about harming yourself? How has your mood been over the last month? Your keyworker says you've been isolating yourself a bit recently. Have you been experiencing any voices? Yes? Can you tell us what they're saying? Internal or external voices? Male or female? Are they commanding? No, good.

Hi, obviously you know me, I'm Claire your CPN. When I gave you your last injection you seemed a bit unsettled – even aggressive, I thought – like you didn't want it. I was a bit worried because it says in your notes that there was an issue with female nurse once? Can you tell us what happened?

Hi, how you doing? Steve, alcohol and drug services. In charge of your methadone script. The pharmacy told us you didn't pick up your script on two occasions last week? I've got to remind you that if you miss three days, you'll have to go through titration again which can take up to two weeks. I've also got some information here about some group work we're asking everyone to take part in as part of their recovery. Every Wednesday afternoon for two hours at Phoenix House. If you don't attend, we'll have to look at your willingness to engage I'm afraid, after all we're all here to look out for the best for you.

12 What is a PIE?

> *Hi – let me introduce myself, I'm Tom, wellbeing adviser. I've been given you to work with because it was flagged that you may be at risk of returning to hospital and calling the ambulance too often, and of course nobody wants that. My job is to help you find some meaningful activities to engage in, OK? Good. Is there anything you like to do? Anything from when you were younger that you would like to revisit? I'll be popping in and talking to your keyworker to try to figure something out, OK? Good.*

So, we must ask, how did our resident end up needing so many workers?

> *He has mild learning difficulties and suffers from anxiety and PTSD due to the abuse he has suffered. He was taken from his family who were physically abusive and neglectful and put into care. In the children's home he was sexually abused. He became mistrustful of services, and abusive to others himself. He left care with no qualifications and had his first psychotic episode at 17 after over using amphetamines. He was diagnosed with paranoid schizophrenia after a second episode later that year which had led to his first of many six-month sections. He had tried to take his own life three times before he was 20 and was hospitalised after cutting his forearm to the bone with a craft knife. He was diagnosed with borderline personality disorder. His chaotic behaviour led to a three-year prison sentence, the first of a number of sentences he has received for low-level anti-social disruptive crimes. He began to use heroin. He didn't have many life skills and was evicted from a number of tenancies due to drug use and debt. He became homeless. After his health started to fail – a product of rough sleeping, poor diet, drug use, and alcohol use – he was given a place at a hostel.*
>
> *This resident is known as RB in emails.*
>
> *A paranoid schizophrenic with anxiety and PTSD. An adult survivor of abuse. An alcoholic. A heroin addict. An abuser. A victim. A history of suicide attempts. A past risk of exploitation. A risk to females. A revolving door client. An individual experiencing severe and enduring mental illness. Non-concordant. A history of carrying a knife. Terrible index forensic crime. A service user. Chaotic. Disordered. Homeless. Volatile. Substance abuser.*
>
> *This is Rob. He was abused as a child.*

Rob's complex needs have led to a formidable array of workers, assessments, and diagnoses. He is framed through his psychiatric care, physical health needs, substance use, and criminal activity, each service's assessment compounding a largely negative set of characteristics and flaws. There are reams of paperwork about Rob, designed to help, but incidentally distancing him from living his own authentic experience.

Rogers states: 'Individuals have within themselves vast resources for self-understanding and for altering their self-concepts, basic attitudes, and self-directed behaviour; these resources can be tapped if a definable climate of facilitative psychological attitudes can be provided.'[9]

Put more simply, our purpose in a PIE care home is to find ways to use ourselves and our environment to help Rob just be Rob.

The PIE models

Foreshadowed by the Enabling Environment standards[10] the PIE principles are an operational framework that can apply to a wide range of human service environments – 'hospital wards, schools, care homes, even some prisons'.[11]

The model is separated into five key areas, or elements, which relate to improving the environment or workers' practice; these five areas are bound by and support two fundamental PIE principles – to build trusting relationships aided by the use of reflective practice.

Without these two principles as the foundation, the model will not function: 'the centrality of building relationships [is to be] treated not as a side issue, but as one of the most pervasive issues that . . . runs through everything'.[12]

The PIE initiative is an evolving process, and at the time of writing there are two PIE models – an 'original formula' PIE and PIE 2.0 – there have also been discussions around introducing two more key areas of 'client participation' and 'access to psychological therapy'.[13]

Both the original and PIE 2.0 model use five key elements, with the PIE 2.0 model providing a slightly looser definition of what it means to be a PIE.

The five key elements

Original Formula	PIE 2.0
Developing a psychological framework	Psychological awareness
Staff training and support	Staff training and support
The environment and social spaces	Spaces of opportunity
Evidence of outcomes	Learning and enquiry
Managing relationships	The 3 Rs – rules, roles, and responsiveness

The five elements in each model can be seen to be very similar, the most notable change being that 'relationships' has now been moved to become

14 *What is a PIE?*

one of the two core principles instead of being one of the five elements, leaving room for the 3 Rs in PIE 2.0.

Pielink.net provides the reasoning behind these changes in detail, but using this table we can see that there has been a move away, for example, from one single 'Psychological Framework' in the original formula to a more general 'Psychological Awareness' in PIE 2.0. This change occurred because a single lens or framework, in practice, was not always desirable or possible. On Psychological frameworks, Pielink.net states:

> 'Some have taken this to mean: being "informed" by a specific approach derived from research of clinical psychology. Others argue that what was originally meant was a recognition of the complex "psychology" of our clients, and so terms like "emotional intelligence" or "active empathy" would have been equally accurate and perhaps more generally applicable.
>
> Some prefer still more specific concepts in psychology, such as "trauma" . . . or specific methods, such as cognitive behavioural therapy, psycho-dynamic insights etc. Others have argued that a much wider perspective is needed (and in most cases, is what is actually used), including "psycho-social" factors, occupational psychology, even anthropology, systems theory. There are certainly many who are trying to make an economic case for recognising the importance of "psychology".
>
> In practice, whatever the chosen formal "approach" – even if there is one – most services and most staff are, in the language of psychological models, "eclectic" – that is, they draw on a wide range of insights and techniques, both for the "culture" of the service as a whole, and for the response to any one individual or incident.'[14]

Another change is from the original to PIE 2.0 formula is 'The Environment' to 'Spaces of Opportunity'. This was altered in recognition that a lot of PIE work is (remembering it has been largely used in homeless provision) happening through outreach or away from built environments.[15]

With the care home being such a well-defined built environment, it makes sense for this element to remain 'original' as: 'designing and managing the social environment is central to developing a psychologically informed service. Thoughtful design. . . . Based on thinking through the intentions behind a service, can result in useful changes in the way a building is used, and how it is valued by staff and clients.'[16]

Similarly, a move to 'Learning and Enquiry' from 'Evidence' in PIE 2.0 might suit some services, but in the heavily regulated care home, with the expectation of audits and paper trails, it is 'Evidence', and concentrating on how we collect it, which most suits our remit.

PIE-R

As this book relates to one care home's journey towards becoming a PIE, this book introduces the model which we used at Highwater House – a hybrid of the two PIE models. I must stress therefore that this is not 'the' PIE model, rather it is 'a' PIE model adapted to suit our needs in the registered care setting. I urge the reader to search for examples of how other services – homeless services, outreach services, and housing services – have used the model; some have omitted areas, some have added areas to suit their particular remit. That the model can be adapted to so many types of human services is a credit to its versatility.

The Psychologically Informed Environment – Residential (PIE-R) model used is:

- **P**sychological awareness
- **E**vidence gathering
- **E**nvironment
- **R**ules, roles, and responsiveness, and
- **S**taff support and training

These five elements are bound by:

- **R**elationships, and
- **R**eflective practice

Using the model

Over the coming chapters each element of the PIE-R model will be explored in detail, using real-world examples and case studies from Highwater House. At the end of each chapter there is a reflection of how the element can support the service, using the outstanding characteristics in the KLOES as a guide.

Notes

1 Rogers, C. R., *On Becoming a Human* (Constable, 2004), 74.
2 www.lexico.com
3 Robin Johnson, co-author of 'psychologically informed services for homeless people' good practice guide 2012. department of communities and local gov. and developer of pielink.net

4 Keats, H., et al., 2012, 5, sourced from https://eprints.soton.ac.uk/340022/1/ Good%2520practice%2520guide%2520-%2520%2520Psychologically%2520 informed%2520services%2520for%2520homeless%2520people%2520.pdf
5 Cockersell, P. (Ed.), *Social Exclusion, Compound Trauma and Recovery* (Jessica Kingsley Publishers, 2018), 221.
6 Herman, J., *Trauma and Recovery* (Basic Books, 1997), 160.
7 Sourced from www.ncbi.nlm.nih.gov/pmc/articles/PMC2791894/
8 Herman, *Trauma and Recovery*, 135.
9 Rogers, C. R., *Way of Being* (Boston: Houghton Mifflin, 1980), 115–117, sourced from www.goodtherapy.org/learn-about-therapy/types/person-centered
10 Enabling Environments standards found at www.rcpsych.ac.uk/docs/default-source/improving-care/ccqi/quality-networks/enabling-environments-ee/ee-standards-document-2015.pdf?sfvrsn=abdcca36_2
11 Levy, J. S. (Ed.) with Johnson, R., *Cross-Cultural Dialogues on Homelessness: From Pretreatment Strategies to Psychologically Informed Environments* (Loving Healing Press, 2017), 163.
12 http://pielink.net/the-three-rs/
13 Cockersell, *Social Exclusion, Compound Trauma and Recovery*, 97.
14 http://pielink.net/questions/a-single-model/
15 http://pielink.net/spaces-of-opportunity/
16 Keats et al., sourced from https://eprints.soton.ac.uk/340022/1/Good%2520 practice%2520guide%2520-%2520%2520Psychologically%2520informed%2520 services%2520for%2520homeless%2520people%2520.pdf

3 Trauma-Informed Care

> In this chapter we will:
>
> - Discover Trauma-Informed Care to be a key psychological lens
> - Be introduced to the types of trauma
> - Explore how the mental health system can create and reinforce trauma
> - Discover how experiences can compound trauma
> - Be introduced to the Adverse Childhood Experience questionnaire

I was talking to Joe, an intensely troubled young man, who was struggling to contain his behaviour. He was extremely confrontational and, as a very imposing individual, regularly used his physicality to intimidate staff. He had a routine of starting with low-level disruption, accusing staff of injecting or poisoning him, before working up to more aggressive confrontation. Today he was unusually willing, or able, to have a direct conversation.

We began to talk about images he often referred to when he was confronting staff: of seeing people who had been attacked with knives and shot; people with machetes coming towards him on the street; of traumatised bodies; and 'gangster' violence. The team had always viewed this as an attempt to portray himself as a gang member, of someone with status, however this conversation with Joe changed my perspective.

Joe said he had spent some time, months, when he was younger seeing gang violence everywhere – he spoke candidly about the sight of mutilated bodies and the visions of gunshot wounds. He was open enough, with gentle prompting, to talk about how anxious this had made him, how scared he was to have been on the streets witnessing these atrocities. His words were full of pain. It was clear, in this moment, that this wasn't the language of intimidation, but of fear.

> With further questioning he told me he had been sectioned for the first time not long after this, and yet the hallucinatory experience of seeing such violence remained very real to him; the memories of this psychosis were traumatic.

In her seminal work *Trauma and Recovery*, Judith Herman explores the trauma that war, abuse, and domestic violence causes and the emotional, physical, and social upheaval and distress that trauma survivors suffer. Joe, too, had experienced a sort of war.

As we have discovered, for us to become a PIE we must place clients' pasts, feelings, and emotions at the forefront of our care delivery. Trauma-Informed Care (TIC) supports this premise and provides the clearest narrative, or lens, through which to understand and work with people's behaviour. This chapter explores TIC and how it can be used in a care home.

For Joe to be helped he needed to have his experience validated. The breakthrough symptoms of his psychosis – what he had seen – continued to drive his feelings of anxiety and fear which needed to be grounded. Whilst anti-psychotic medication could stop these hallucinations it did not mean that the painful emotional memories that he had were also erased, and, as they remained in him, were a huge point of trauma and dislocation, affecting his daily mood and informing his behaviour.

We know from social services reports that Joe's life before this psychotic break had been fraught with drug use and low social standing. Being sectioned and subsumed into the mental health services further disempowered and isolated him; Herman writes that psychological trauma is an affliction of the powerless.[1] By the time he came to Highwater, many years after this first episode, Joe had become a revolving door patient, well known for his threatening behaviour and mistrust of services. His life had become a series of negative events, each compounding prior negative experiences. Regularly moving from acute ward to tenancy, to supported housing, he became a transient service user. As the risk assessments about him grew, his options became more limited. His willingness to physically attack any figure of authority, his disregard for others' rights to safety, and confrontational attitude led to further isolation; every engagement became a wary and fraught experience for both Joe and the workers, with potentially harmful outcomes. He had, over a period of years, lost the ability to trust what was real and the capacity to feel grounded, and had become reliant on a system which invoked in him paranoia and isolation. Joe's story shows that interacting with the system itself can be traumatic.[2]

Joe's needs were unable to be met by the intervention of a psychiatric medical model; the system is not designed to support the social and emotional needs of such a traumatised individual. It focuses on crisis resolution and working with *ill*-health, rather than promoting wider interventions in mental health, or working with the social and emotional implications of traumatic experience. Despite an increasing use of the recovery model, austerity budgets have led to cuts in many outreach teams across the UK and an absence of good-quality, well-resourced community teams leading to delayed discharge from hospitals and an increase in reports of poorer community services.[3]

This focus on curing faulty brain chemistry through use of medication, and the inference therefore that the unwell individual is the broken part of the equation does not allow for a wider conversation around how the environment can be supportive, curative, and grounding, or destructive, isolating, and inhibiting. The relatively clinical setting of a mental health ward places the patient in a passive role, one of being done 'to'. This submissive state does not allow for the patient to affect their environment, a state of doing 'with', which erodes their self-efficacy. In Joe's story this had led to a cycle of dependency and distrust with each placement failure.

There is, implicit in the medical model, a supposition of a baseline of 'normality', an undefined state of wellbeing that can be returned to, if only the correct medication regime is used. This model does not cater for those who have little 'normality' to return to, people who have never known a secure base or felt a sense of personal equilibrium. Trauma survivors who have been through the psychiatric system may of course benefit from medication, and crisis intervention is often necessary, but it cannot and does not provide a complete answer – there are social side effects to mental illness and use of the psychiatric system which medication cannot cure. To put it another way, you cannot medicate memories, and memories affect behaviour.

Trauma and abuse

Traumatic experiences can be separated into two groups known as type I and type II trauma. Here we look at these definitions and reflect on the effects they can have on a person.

In the 18 years that I have worked at Highwater House a great number of people who have come through our doors have witnessed and/or been abused as children, although we are not a specialist unit in this area. Of the 22 residents living here today, 18 (80%) are survivors of childhood abuse, and this figure remains consistent as I look back through our past residents. Every person carries a personal story, yet their histories have similar themes of a life of disruption, insecurity, isolation, and helplessness, typical in trauma survivors. These feelings, it is clear, have often been compounded and magnified as they are pushed through 'the system', leading to low trust in professionals and feelings of anger, resentment, and shame. That this percentage of survivors of abuse is so consistently high amongst our resident population confirms studies which show homelessness, substance use, and poor mental health are common symptoms of a traumatic childhood,[4] Gabor Maté writes that addicts are not born, but made.[5] Survivors of abuse – people who have grown up in chronically unsafe surroundings – will often be hypervigilant, untrusting, and impulsive. Evans and Coccoma explain:

> studies show that the inability to escape chronic fear and feelings of helplessness can cause long term damage in the emotion regulating systems in the brain and impede the ability to apply logical thought to the intense emotions traumatic memories invoke.[6]

As their secure attachments and boundaries are repeatedly violated the individual finds it increasingly hard to regulate their emotions. Their attentional bias understandably sees threat beyond 'usual' parameters – as an adult survivor of abuse this threat could, for example, be seen in the benign actions of a carer, or an environment, such as a care home.

Herman named this chronic state of anxiety 'type II' trauma, and it is the effects of this catastrophic condition which we, in a PIE and working with tri-morbidity, must remain acutely aware of, and be prepared to work with.

Type I trauma refers to a single traumatic incident, for example a car crash or single incident of rape, rather than the prolonged and repeated exposure as defined by type II trauma. The response to a type I traumatic incident will therefore differ to the way we respond to type II trauma. If, for example, we are supporting someone who has been in a car crash, we wouldn't presume their sense of self had been decayed by years of coercive and controlling behaviour. Our response would be appropriate for the incident.

Many of our residents at Highwater have experienced both type I and type II trauma; the tragedy of childhood abuse often creates a spiral of events leading to ever more layers of trauma. As these incidents combine within the person, they create complex, or compound, trauma.

> *Abused physically by her mother and sexually by her father as a child, Beth was born into a life of chronic trauma. Now, as a 50-year-old woman, she lives in a highly anxious state, easily manipulated and extorted, who regulates her emotions through crack and heroin use. Hers has been a lifetime of longing for stability, yet her impulsive and chaotic behaviour have not allowed for this. This perpetuating cycle of isolation, drug use and oscillation between attachment and defiance has led to her street working, living with abusive partners, multiple overdoses and numerous mental health sections. She has lived through*

a range of traumatic incidents: the death of a partner who overdosed; psychotic episodes where she has woken up thinking someone has been in her room and bashed her head against the wall; belief that people are following her with knives; she has been beaten and abused on the street; and felt emotionally torn by her inability to remain 'loved' by someone. When Beth feels upset, she will chase staff about the home and stand in the middle of the room stamping her feet much like a young child having a tantrum. She often screams and becomes hysterical for seemingly little reason, with small problems blowing up into great emotional storms.

Her inability to sustain intimate relationships and establish safe and appropriate boundaries is a common facet of survivors,[7] she also embodies a 'lack of verbal and social skills for resolving conflict . . . [approaching] problems with the expectation of hostile attack';[8] her behaviour is similar to that of a small child unable to cope with the forces of the world around her. Someone with little control over their destiny.

Recognising Beth's difficulty to protect herself emotionally as a symptom of childhood trauma, and seeing her often demanding behaviour not as disruptive but deregulated has given the staff team confidence to respond to her needs in a proactive way. They became more reassuring, and took more time to empower Beth to make authentic connections with them; empowering individuals in a community setting is a cornerstone of both TIC and PIE.

Using a psychologically informed approach has improved our ability – that is, understanding of how to – work with individuals with compound trauma such as Beth. I'm pleased to say that whilst three years ago Beth was regularly injecting heroin and overdosing, often needing to be revived or the ambulance called (six times in 2016, five times in 2017), she has since stopped using heroin intravenously and has not overdosed for almost two years. She has also not been sectioned or arrested, and she rarely street works. She is, rather, a lively member of the home's community, still with ups and downs, but better able to self-soothe and trust her environment.

ACEs

A tool to help us recognise whether someone has experienced trauma is the Adverse Childhood Experience (ACE) questionnaire. Readily available online, there are ten questions based around abuse, neglect, and household dysfunction in childhood (up to 18 years old). The higher the score, the greater the risk of future health problems, including symptoms of trauma. Repeated studies show there is a direct link between childhood trauma and adult onset of chronic disease, as well as depression, suicide, and being violent or a victim of violence. The more types of trauma witnessed increases the risk of health, social, and emotional problems.[9] The questionnaire does not consider positive experiences in childhood which could help build resilience or other coping life skills, and so has its faults, however, it is useful as a guide to recognising traumatic experiences in clients. A score of four or more means a person's risk greatly increases around substance use and alcoholism, suicide and mental health issues: at Highwater house our residents average a score of four, with some individuals' scores being much higher.

The long-term effects of childhood trauma, abuse, and neglect cannot be over-estimated; the social, emotional, and economic implications affect us all. The rupture that takes place in the child's life can be devastating, with life-long consequences.

Children's homes and prison

It is notable that an increasing number of our residents have spent time in the care system as children, and for this reason often have knowledge of, and mistrust, the system that they are re-entering as adults. They are generally deeply suspicious of the relationships offered and feel a great deal of shame at their inability to cope on their own. When this is the case, we should be especially aware of the resident playing out old relationships and placing the carers in particular roles.

Research by the National Society for the Prevention of Cruelty to Children has found that on average there are between 250 and 300 cases of confirmed abuse in residential care every year. In residential care the rate of substantiated abuse claims is significantly higher than for foster families, with an average of between two and three proven cases per 100 children:[10] it is a sad reality that, in my experience, most residents who have been in care as children will have some experience of abuse, either directly or indirectly. That they have been taken into state care inevitably means the child will have witnessed and lived through some traumatic incidents.

We must therefore presume the worst if someone has been in a children's home, and expect there to be symptoms of trauma – disconnection from others and disempowerment – caused either before or during their stay in care. As we move through the key areas introducing the PIE model into a specific care setting, we will remain particularly mindful of the power imbalance inherent in a care home, and reflect on the memories of helplessness that adults may have of their childhood in care.

Equally we must stay aware of the effects that incarceration will have had upon them. Petty crime, drug use, and 'street' behaviour will have led our residents to incidents of conflict with the police and judiciary. This will have added to feelings of hopelessness and helplessness within them, of being an outsider and feeling abused by the system. The paranoia rife within this client group creates a tribal belief that any authority is automatically hostile and will be a restrictive force on their freedom to self-medicate – which it often is.

Of 22 residents currently living at Highwater House, every single one has been detained under the Mental Health Act. Every single one has been arrested and 19 out of 22 have been in prison – trauma is a certainty, as is anger and shame.

Responding to trauma

Incorporating trauma-informed practice into our care ensures our residents, openly suffering or otherwise, receive the best care we can offer. As we move further through this book it is TIC principles that guide our best practice as we introduce the PIE principles.

It is therefore helpful to introduce the key aims of trauma-informed intervention. These are to:

- Promote a sense of safety
- Promote calm
- Promote a sense of self-efficacy and collective efficacy
- Promote connectedness
- Instil hope[11]

Herman writes:

> The core experiences of psychological trauma are disempowerment and disconnection from others. Recovery, therefore, is based upon the empowerment of the survivor and the creation of new connections. Recovery can only take place within the context of relationships; it cannot occur in isolation. In her renewed connections with other people, the survivor re-creates the psychological faculties that were damaged or deformed by the traumatic experience. These faculties include the basic capacities for trust, autonomy, initiative, competence, identity, and intimacy.[12]

We can see that the foundations for providing care for traumatised people like Joe and Beth are in many ways quite simple. Calm and supportive relationships are the bedrock of working in a PIE and of TIC. As the person affects and is affected by their environment, they can begin to exert some control and enact positive change. Supporting and developing this self-efficacy in residents is a central goal of PIE workers; by accepting that traumatic experience has left them both anxiously in need and angrily dismissive gives us the tools to help support them negotiate this dilemma.

This is not deep therapeutic work only able to be done by a psychiatrist or specialist, rather it is human connection done skilfully; our traumatised residents, above all, need trustable relationships borne from kindness, honesty, awareness of need, and compassion.

This of course deeply resonates with the carers' role, and presents the care home as a unique opportunity to fulfil the residents' needs – socially and emotionally; that is, relationally.

The twin strands of TIC and PIE provide a road map answering the complex questions posed by residents who have lived through abusive pasts, have ongoing substance use issues, and difficulty in maintaining placements. I would urge the reader to further explore TIC, and to encourage managers to provide training in this area. In my opinion it is a necessity for PIE staff to have a rudimentary understanding of TIC for them to truly grasp the life-long implications of compound trauma and the effects it wields upon individuals.

Both the PIE and TIC principles place building relationships as the central theme of recovery. Over the next chapter we explore how this relates to working in a care home.

This chapter has reflected KLOE:

S1

- 'The service is particularly creative in the ways it involves and works with people to understand their diverse circumstances and individual needs.'

C3

- 'The service anticipates people's needs and recognises distress and discomfort at the earliest stage. It offers respectful and supportive care.'

Notes

1 Herman, J., *Trauma and Recovery* (Basic Books, 1997), 33.
2 Goodman et al., 1991, seen in a PowerPoint delivered at Homeless link conference 2019.
3 Sourced from www.kingsfund.org.uk/sites/default/files/field/field_publication_file/mental-health-under-pressure-nov15_0.pdf pg8

4 www.gov.im/media/1350678/homeless-stats-uk.pdf
5 Maté, G., *In the Realm of the Hungry Ghosts* (Vermillion, 2018), 259.
6 LeDoux, J. E., (2000) Emotion circuits in the brain, *Annual Review of Neuroscience*, 23: 155–184, Van der Kolk, B. A., (2006) Clinical implications of neuroscience research in PTSD, *Annals New York Academy of Sciences*, 1071: 277–293, Evans, A. and Coccoma, P., *Trauma-informed Care: How Neuroscience Influences Practice* (Routledge, 2016), 29.
7 Herman, *Trauma and Recovery*, 111.
8 Herman, *Trauma and Recovery*, 104.
9 Found at www.acesconnection.com/blog/got-your-ace-resilience-scores
10 www.independent.co.uk/news/uk/crime/major-study-reveals-true-scale-of-abuse-of-children-living-in-care-9587244.html
11 Evans and Coccoma, *Trauma-informed Care*, 17.
12 Herman, *Trauma and Recovery*, 133.

4 Relationships

> In this chapter we will:
>
> - Discover relationships to be at the heart of the PIE framework
> - Explore behaviour as a form of communication
> - Explore how trauma can impede relationship building
> - See the care home as a unique environment to engage marginalised clients
> - Explore language as a key aspect of building good relationships

Forging strong relationships and reflective practice together form the backbone to any Psychologically Informed Environment. Relationships are the beating heart to the approach – everything else – work practice, staff behaviour and intentions – coalesces around the connections the worker makes with the resident.

Positive relationships are cited throughout the Key Lines of Enquiry prompts and characteristics as an important aspect of enabling good care, and to creating a person-centred approach. Strong relationships support residents to receive dignified care, free from abuse, in a safe environment, as stated in the fundamental standards. Valued relationships will shine through during any inspection and clearly show the service is providing person-centred, respectful care by fit and proper staff.

In a recent CQC inspection report Highwater House was commended for the staff's strong relationships with residents noting:

> the service promoted a kind, caring and empathetic culture using a new initiative Psychological Informed Environment (PIE) approach. This approach aims to reduce social exclusion and improve the mental health

of homeless people. It also aims to improve staff morale and encourage positive interaction. PIE puts the relationships staff develop with people at the very heart of the care process.[1]

Becoming a PIE and placing the relationships between worker and resident so centrally gave a new, more empathic voice to the service and undoubtedly helped the service improve from being the solid 'good' provision of previous inspections to becoming outstanding.

Forging relationships

The PIE approach relies on workers' willingness to reach out and use themselves – their interpersonal skills – as the tool through which the client can change their lives for the better. Rogers explains: 'If I can provide a certain type of relationship, the other person will discover within himself the capacity to use that relationship for growth, and change and personal development will occur'[2] – the worker then, is the lightning rod for the client's self-defeating behaviour, and the conduit through which they can enact change. The emotional value the worker places upon their interactions with residents fuels belief that change is manageable and possible. A key principle of Trauma-Informed Care is that relationships are integral to healing trauma – indeed, that recovery can only take place in the context of relationships.[3]

As workers place themselves in this supportive role, they must be a willing and an aware participant in the ensuing tussle of transference and countertransference, remaining alert to their influence upon the client, and accepting that the client will also affect them. The PIE approach asks a lot of workers: to question and challenge their influence on the environment, to become creative and more flexible in their care giving, and to be reflective about their own needs and expectations, both individually and as a representative of a service. The outcome of these demands will however be positive – the worker will become more confident in challenging situations; their sense of purpose bolstered as previously unreachable, unmanageable clients become engaged. They will feel supported and skilled in their workplace, certain that their work practice is having a positive effect on clients' lives. The strength born from well-formed relationships is holistic and protective for both client and worker.

This psychodynamic alliance – the shared narrative between resident and worker – can become a source of hope and resilience for a person experiencing the full force of addiction. As part of the resident's complex response to a lifetime of traumatic experiences, mental ill-health, and social isolation, addiction is a product of an attempt to find safety – using substances to self-medicate intolerable feelings. Residents will know they're causing more damage and pain to themselves as they use drugs, and yet will do so to alleviate their psychological pain in the short term.[4] They will be cycling through a life script where self-preservation is procured through anti-social behaviour – using aggression to keep people at arm's length – and a dysfunctional homeostasis is attained through their drug use. They will be disconnected from their life story and exhausted from the daily struggle of keeping the worst of life at bay. Time and again at Highwater House we have witnessed residents come through the door determined to keep these defences in place, their only certainty being that to feel safe must also mean being, in any deeply connected sense, alone. Well-attuned relationships will help counter this distress and help to create hope; for hope plays an integral role in motivation for growth beyond trauma.[5]

Behaviour as communication

Humans are inherently social creatures with an urge to create connections, yet trauma and adverse life experiences can lead people to become isolated and mistrustful of support. As negative life events compound one another, the person can become disjointed from normal behaviour – so perpetuating a cycle of detachment. Survivors of abuse often lack verbal and social skills for resolving conflict, and they approach problems with the expectation of hostile attack.[6] A PIE worker should assume their challenging resident has experienced trauma in their past, and that their anti-social behaviour is a form of communication. This may be a confusing experience for both worker and resident at times, however with improved psychological awareness, the worker will be able to assist the resident to express their needs in a more acceptable manner. By being the constant in the equation, the resident has a reliable point of reflection.

> *David is a deeply troubled individual. He came to the home after being found sleeping rough and eating out of bins, and, at 58, suffers from a number of physical health problems and is a chronic drinker. David can be a charming, reflective character when he's sober and feels comfortable, however these strengths are overshadowed by anti-social behaviour. David finds it difficult to communicate his needs and, due to his relentless alcohol consumption, often becomes confused and lives in the moment. Upon moving into Highwater House, David's initial attempts at expressing his needs and asking for help were by any standards dysfunctional. When he perceived that his needs were not going to be met – as was historically true – he showed his frustration through acts of self-sabotage and aggression. He communicated his fear and anxiety by shouting at*

staff, kicking the office door, urinating on the office door and defecating in the foyer on the floor.

Staff accepted that David's desire to be cared for and fear of being further neglected led him to behave like this. His needs were great and it became apparent that from a young age and throughout his life he had been left to fend for himself. He had been abused by his primary carers as a small boy and had never had a successful relationship. He began drinking as a teen – self-medicating against the effects of the trauma he had suffered. He had learned that being aggressive not only kept people (potential abusers) away but it also meant that often his basic needs would be met. He found that shouting and being intimidating made people respond to him and give him what he demanded – as a tall man he could use his presence to instil fear and get food, medication, or attention. He had spent most of his life in this duality of being fearful and creating fear in others and his extreme behaviours ensured he was always marginalised. His learnt behaviour that kept him safe was ultimately self-defeating and isolating.

By seeing David's anti-social behaviour as a form of communication staff could re-frame these issues as a conversation. They told him directly his needs would always be met at the home and created a trusting bond, shown through their actions, that this was true. They set reasonable boundaries regarding acceptable behaviour around the home and used their approachable, unflappable demeanour to talk them through with him. Through consistency and patience David began to have faith that his needs could and would be met. His anxiety receded as his relationship with staff and the environment solidified. His communication became more nuanced – he stopped protesting through defecation and urinating and started to use a more considered, verbal approach to attaining his needs.

David continues to struggle with expressing himself – his use of alcohol and lifetime of entrenched behaviour and poor coping mechanisms leads him to have angry outbursts as he wrestles with the internal battles his life has left him with. He is, however, now warm, well fed and feels able to trust the service and staff. The building of relationships and the acceptance of David's difficulties has meant he is safer than ever before.

This case study shows that through building rapport with David, and the workers proving themselves to be consistent and trustable, helped him to change his way of communicating for the better. Opening a supportive dialogue with David and adhering to a script that his fears (of being neglected) would not be realised led him to feeling settled. The relationship fostered between the staff and David was the conduit through which this behavioural change could take place.

Emotional algebra

The *Oxford English Dictionary* defines relationships as: 'the way in which two or more people or things are connected, or the state of being connected'. Place a person in any environment and they are in inextricably in relation to it, put a person next to a person, or a pencil next to a pencil – they are, and cannot *not* be, seen in relation to each other. With this inevitability of relationships being driven by proximity there can only be one question to ask as a PIE worker. How will I use this relationship, this closeness, to enhance the outcomes for those involved? The worker, as the paid professional, has a responsibility to reflect upon this, and as the most powerful part of the 'relationship equation' should be mindful of the effect their actions have upon the others in the relationship.

Whilst relationships can be both 'good' (their relationship was wonderful) or 'bad' (their relationship broke down), positive or negative, one thing is absolute, all relationships have value of some sort. They cannot exist in a vacuum – relationships demand attention. Neglected relationships are jarring and burgeoning relationships are exciting.

> *Relationships can be seen as an equation of many parts with each element reliant upon and affecting the others. A well-ordered 'relationship equation' will be balanced with variables offset by constants and numbers that make sense of operators. Humans have an innate skill to balance 'relationship equations', knowing when to add to and subtract from different areas of their relationship experience, and how to balance themselves within the wider 'equation'. This skill can, however, be stunted by experiences of trauma.*
>
> *The traumatised person has fully or partially lost the ability to do 'emotional algebra' but is still part of the equation and expected to take part as a fully-fledged 'mathematician'.*
>
> *To this person the numbers make no sense, they add too much on one side and it all comes crashing down, they take too much from the other and the same happens. It becomes more and more frustrating and confused the more they try to find ways to solve this very real emotional mess.*
>
> *They might try getting angry and attempt to kick the equation apart or try to erase it by taking obliterating levels of drugs, but it is always there, immovable and unresolved.*
>
> *To solve any equation there is always a need for a constant.*

> Without a constant the equation is a collection of random unsolvable quantities. The PIE worker can be that much needed figure, providing perspective and certainty to the rest of the 'equation', and re-teaching the rules of 'emotional algebra'.
>
> A trustable, consistent point that the service user can use to begin to understand, reflect on, and re-evaluate the other aspects of their life, that is, to start solving the equation.

Relationships in a care environment are inevitable; the relationship between service providers and service users, peer relationships, the relationship between resident and environment – all play a part in shaping the care the client receives and accepts.

Trauma and relationships

The workers therefore must reflect on the residents' prior experience of relationships and the likelihood that they may not have had many, if any, positive or 'normal' relationships to draw from. They may respond to the offer of friendship in erratic, aggressive, or dismissive ways, uncertain how to behave and fearful of the trust a positive relationship promises.

The inherent power imbalance within the carer/cared for dynamic can be debilitating to the resident. Trauma can create in people dramatic responses to being offered care and support. They may find it difficult to establish safe or appropriate boundaries – they might become overly attached, or acutely defensive. Herman writes of the trauma survivor: 'her empathic atonement to the wishes of others and her automatic, often unconscious habit of obedience make her vulnerable to anyone in a position of power or authority'.[7]

It is well known that childhood trauma can interfere with the natural ability to form bonds.[8] As the ripples of trauma are felt throughout the person's life, they become mistrusting adults whose risky and isolating behaviour compounds previous trauma, and whose acute vulnerability leaves them open to further abuse.

Our early years contain the processes that are key to living as a successful adult – a healthy childhood will provide boundaried care, responsiveness, a feeling of security, and positive regard. A childhood full of adverse experiences compounded by the inability to escape from chronic fear creates dysfunction and feelings of helplessness which can cause long-term damage to the emotion regulating part of the brain – the amygdala. This in turn can impede the ability to apply logical thought to the intense emotions that the traumatic memories evoke,[9] and makes it hard to sustain relationships.

Upon meeting a client and beginning the process of forming a trusting relationship, the worker must be mindful of this and understand what might seem like odd, impulsive, and self-defeating behaviour to be responses to trauma.

Similarly, a resident may not have the emotional literacy needed to express themselves fully and could need guidance to regulate their language. They may seem frustrated or feel angry as the urge to connect with a fellow human is thwarted by their confusion of how to speak and behave in a given situation – their ability to do 'emotional algebra' undeveloped or lost. It is easy then for them to slip into a life-long script, driven by fear of rejection, to say the worker is at fault and is being manipulative – for them to use verbal aggression to remain isolated but, in their eyes, safe.

> *'She can fuck off! I'm never speaking to her again!'*
> *'Who?'*
> *'Amy. She marched straight past me and ignored me – bitch!'*
> *'Are you sure? She might have just not seen you.'*
> *'Nah, you're all like it, too busy and stuck up to even say "hello"! You're just here for the money!'*
>
> *Amy says 'hello' to Pete at least ten times a day and is very kindly towards him, yet his anxiety caused by issues around attachment and rejection doesn't allow him to trust the relationship easily.*
>
> *If he feels at all slighted, or abandoned, he jumps straight into being very aggressive. A defence mechanism against being hurt, and a sign there has been trauma in his past.*

How the worker reacts in this situation is integral to creating a secure base and the positive outcomes this brings. Armed with the knowledge that trauma can elicit hyperarousal, defensiveness, and impulsivity, they can provide for the resident an opportunity to experiment with relationship building and hope, helping them edge further away from the deep mistrust they feel towards others. As the relationship is repeatedly proved through consistency and stability, they can begin to trust that they will not be harmed by the closeness it brings.

For the worker this process can be a rewarding but tiring experience demanding continuous reflection upon the residents and their own behaviour. However, the knowledge that supportive relationships are identified as key to trauma recovery should spur them on to remain stoic in the face of a difficult bonding process and certain that their actions are having an effect. Cockersell sums this up neatly with: 'if trauma results from bad experiences and damaging relationships, then healing arises from positive relationships and good experiences'.[10]

This trusting bond which promotes resilience, hope and self-worth is, in essence, the therapeutic alliance of Carl Rogers' work.

The therapeutic alliance

Rogers, the father of person-centred therapy, believed there are three core conditions needed for positive therapeutic change to take place and whilst frontline PIE workers are explicitly not counsellors, these values resonate in any care-giving relationship.

His three conditions are:

- Congruence
- Unconditional positive regard and
- Empathy

Taken together these are the foundation of a successful progressive, 'helping' relationship.

Congruence means genuineness. For a worker to be open and clear, that is, authentic, about their abilities to support the resident is to not create false hope or feelings of abandonment, an important part of creating a secure base. Genuineness also helps protect the worker and client from falling into a pattern of negative projection or projective identification – where troubled people place feelings they can't accept in themselves onto others and their environment – which can lead to a culture of blame and feelings of anger. Responding authentically to residents is an important aspect of building a trusting bond, especially in an environment with an inherent power imbalance such as a care home.

Unconditional positive regard means accepting the resident for who they are even if the worker does not agree with some of the residents' choices or actions. The often baffling, self-destructive behaviour of traumatised, addicted individuals can leave the worker frustrated and disorientated. Anyone who has worked in this field will have asked themselves a number of times: 'how can a resident who was doing so well do something so clearly self-harming?'

Placing unconditional positive regard at the centre of relationship building, and using the PIE framework to provide a lens through which to see possible reasons as to why a client might behave destructively, helps protect the worker and support the resident to feel validated as a person. The resident will know that their behaviour is self-harming, and will be feeling shameful about some of their actions. If they feel judged by the workers in their home, they will not take part in a relationship, rather they will have their suspicions that they are 'bad' people confirmed. Survivors of abuse often feel they are to blame for what happened to them with their self-esteem assaulted by feelings of humiliation – any behaviour by the worker that can be interpreted as disgust or dislike is likely to trigger these entrenched feelings of guilt and helplessness.[11]

Showing people unconditional positive regard is also protective for the worker in an often-volatile emotional landscape. Knowing in yourself that every action and conversation you have been part of has placed the wellbeing and validation of the client at the fore gives a freedom to be honest and for feelings of angst or self-blame around residents' actions to be reduced.

Unconditional positive regard does not, however, involve collusion around anti-social behaviour and drug use – people should be supported to make their own judgements and choices but the worker must remain focussed on providing authentic, honest reflection upon the client's actions. Colluding, supporting, or agreeing with anti-social behaviour will lead to more damaging outcomes for the client as they take their actions to be validated by a carer – someone 'in power'.

Empathy refers to the ability to understand what the client is feeling and, using unconditional regard, to accept it. As an addict or traumatised person is wrestling with feelings they can't cope with, it is of utmost importance that when they do connect emotionally this is acknowledged and responded to. In this way the channels, broken by a life of misdirection and mistrust, can begin to reform or begin to be built.

Rogers (to paraphrase) describes empathy as recognising another's emotional state as if it were your own whilst never losing sight of the 'as if', that is, to sense and frame the other person's feelings successfully without over identifying with it. Over-identification with another's feelings – transference – without sufficient personal resilience or recognition can lead to compassion fatigue and the retraction of care, whilst a lack of empathy will stop a positive relationship from being formed at all. Both states are unwanted, yet perhaps more common than we'd like to admit – especially in an untrained team. A PIE aims to improve the ability of workers to connect with damaged people whilst providing boundaries and guidance to moderate the emotional toil that connection may have.

Empathy is the carer's primary tool – the urge to care is a tremendous character trait and should be tended carefully.

If a PIE worker keeps these tenants at the fore when building relationships, they will help the resident feel authentically supported and able to trust the worker.

What is professionalism?

Over the years I have seen some workers protect themselves by refusing to share any aspect of their home life or past – preferring to use a shield of professionalism to guard themselves from emotional attacks from a traumatised client. Their reasoning for conducting themselves like this may seem watertight – they are behaving professionally. However, this 'hands off' style of care creates a static situation – the helper and helped frozen in their roles. Without introducing tactile emotional language, without a place to dump their despair and hopes, without a safe, trusted space to try out new ways of behaving, without the staff providing a road map to more sustainable friendships away from their drug circle, the care home becomes a holding cell, a place of safety but not of growth. In this situation the staff and resident are complicit in the resident becoming a 'professional patient': the worker and resident in their restrictive identities playing out their isolated roles whilst ostensibly sharing the space. Of course – as we've discovered – no two objects can be in the same space and remain unrelated, and so the likely outcome will be that the resident will ultimately feel dismissed and unwelcomed by the stiff, formal 'professionalism' of the worker.

Conversely, I have also witnessed staff become overly connected with residents – leaving the worker emotionally vulnerable, tired and ultimately unable to do their job well. Trauma is contagious and compassion fatigue real. It is easy to see how this over-empathic support can happen. A naturally caring person supporting a resident they have an affinity with, in a supportive and safe environment, leads to a sense of security and a willing suspension of disbelief for both parties – they both want the resident to be the best version of themselves. Unfortunately, this can mean not fully accepting the trauma the client has been through and the deregulation in their internal landscape. The resident may present as capable of sustaining a more profound in-depth friendship but, in reality, be struggling to keep this façade up. This situation will lead to anger, fear of disappointing the worker, and emotional outbursts. For the worker this behaviour can feel directed at them personally; they may become despondent in their work and feel hurt. The lack of consistency in the relationship as the worker withdraws their care to more sustainable levels become a hindrance to the residents' personal growth and can lead to confusion and anger. This toxic help increases despair and a sense of hopelessness already deeply ingrained in the client.[12]

In both these scenarios the worker feels like they are doing their best to fulfil their role, and yet neither of them is truly succeeding.

To mitigate these damaging situations PIE workers should receive training in working with trauma, and/or attachment theory. As their understanding of the impact of their behaviour improves, so the residents receive better care. Using the PIE approach helps guide and promote informed, mindful actions whilst creating relationships that provide longevity for the client.

Vicarious trauma

In building clear, empathic relationships with traumatised clients the worker can leave themselves open to experiencing vicarious trauma, that is, and taken from the British Medical Associations website, 'a process of change resulting from empathetic engagement with trauma survivors. Anyone who engages empathetically with survivors of traumatic incidents, torture, and material relating to their trauma, is potentially affected, including doctors and other health professionals.'[13]

A PIE worker should not be fearful of experiencing vicarious trauma but should remain mindful of the possibility of it occurring. Later we will see how the PIE framework addresses supporting frontline staff working with traumatised individuals and look at the symptoms of vicarious trauma.

As a trusting bond grows between the resident and carer, so the chance of them sharing stories about their past increases and should be welcomed. This is an integral aspect of their healing process and it is a real breakthrough when they begin to open up. Whereas less chaotic people could access mainstream services at this point – such as a counselling service – dually diagnosed residents often cannot. Their addictions, risk assessment, and anti-social behaviour generally prevent them from successfully passing the inclusion criteria – for example, counsellors will not counsel drunk people; they insist on sobriety at the very time the addict, when exploring their past, is feeling the most pain and most likely to self-medicate. When the relationship is secure enough for them to trust workers, the resident might feel comfortable enough to explore their past trauma – and so the PIE worker must be ready to accept that sharing and bear witness to it with unconditional acceptance and genuine support. Working with marginalised people will often mean frontline staff will be the primary ear to these traumatised individuals – it seems almost unbelievable that someone could have gone through the mental health system and not fully disclosed their trauma or childhood abuse, but it has happened many times at Highwater House where the carer's layman's ear hears the stories that a more clinical ear has not.

Responding with compassion then is key to not further compounding the resident's trauma whilst also remaining aware of one's own responses – it is likely that distressing conversations will lead to unpleasant somatic responses and feelings which should be allowed to surface in supervision sessions or in conversations with other staff.

As the resident shares their story the carer may have a natural urge to try to counsel the upset, confessional resident, but it is imperative to understand that 'doing' therapy badly can be as traumatising as dismissing the conversation. Therapy can 'inadvertently reactivate feelings of self-hate and shame because of the power imbalance between patient and therapist',[14] and in an already skewed relationship in favour of the carer this could have a devastating impact upon the wellbeing of the resident in their own home.

> *Jane, at first meeting, seemed a robust character. She was renowned for being able to 'hold her own', she was talkative and sociable. She was*

happy to say she had had a hard life that had led her to Birmingham where she had used a variety of drugs before returning to Norwich with a methadone script and a six-can-a-day alcohol addiction.

As the weeks passed and Jane settled into the home she would often, in the evening after a lot of alcohol, become disruptive before crying and saying she didn't feel safe. This pattern of behaviour continued for some time – a seemingly competent individual with a destructive bent which came out when she'd been drinking.

Much of Jane's conversation was based in the present. She was very opinionated about other residents and staff, picking out behaviour she wasn't happy with and often complaining about minor things. To this end she was seen as a likeable but relatively troublesome person.

Jane began to trust the staff and the supportive environment. The accessibility of the workers allowed her to feel comfortable that someone was always there to ensure her safety.

One Saturday I was watching television with her in the lounge and she was eating a bag of sweets. She told me her mother used to work in a sweet factory. She went on to say that this was when she was young and her mother would lock Jane and her brother in a room while she went to work nightshifts, which had made Jane fearful of locked doors and worried about fires. At around this time her mother began a relationship with a man who sexually abused Jane for a number of years before going to prison. She spoke openly and earnestly about this for some time, becoming quite animated and engaging me in her story. Jane was taken into care until the age of 16, then returned to her mother's flat where the abuser had returned after serving his sentence. Jane said she was now old enough to stop him from abusing her again, although he tried.

She began to use drugs heavily and ended up in Birmingham. She had a young child taken from her whom Jane misses greatly.

Her life had been one of fear, uncertainty, loss and shame. She felt angry and had found being aggressive and a street drinking 'character' masked and numbed this terrible history.

As we sat and spoke it was clear she hadn't shared this level of information in this style of friendly conversation before – she was talking about her abuse in very emotional terms. The home and I had become a secure base for her and she had become comfortable to try out verbalising and sharing some of her trauma.

I felt a strong duty to respond thoughtfully and clearly. I did not want to tell her 'but you're alright now' as this could dismiss the past, neither did I want to enquire too deeply as it was not a contained therapeutic

> environment. I chose to say she would always be supported at the home to be as open as she felt able and that I would be available to listen. I said I thought that parts of her life story were very sad and that she must feel angry and hurt.
>
> I didn't want to behave like a counsellor, I wanted to behave like a friend – a part of the equation she could trust to be non-judgemental, reliable, and who would not be shocked by her story.

Jane chose to speak out at a wholly innocuous time – there was no suggestion that she would suddenly want to be so open about her past trauma. She obviously felt comfortable in that situation and with our relationship and could use it to release some of her pain.

This is only the first steps for Jane – she has a lifetime of trauma to make sense of, but it was the warmth of human engagement – friendship – and not clinical professionalism that allowed her to open up. This is why relationships are so integral and important to the PIE principles.

Relationships and addiction

Building relationships with addicted people fully entrenched in a cycle of substance use is tough. Swinging chaotically between being accessible and reflective, to having paranoid outbursts or weeks of being in a near catatonic state, the consistency through which a normal relationship develops is rarely present. The mechanisms they use to cope can stop the addict from forming even the most rudimentary emotional connection defined by any 'normal' parameters. Coupled with the mistrust that runs so deeply through clients who are professional patients, there can seem to be little for the worker to gain traction upon within the client to begin the process of forming a relationship.

The addicts' time-line differs from the workers. The cycle of substance use leads to short – daily, or even hourly – focus on the next need for the drug (including alcohol), which takes precedence over all else. The alchoholic's urge to drink, to subdue chronic anxiety, and stop the chance of having a seizure is an all-encompassing job, with binges sometimes lasting for months. During this time the resident will only see as far as the next drink – so making appointments a week or more in advance, and getting annoyed if they don't attend, is a fool's errand. Similarly, the addiction cycle of a crack or heroin user can be a full-time occupation, and so engrossing that even dire health needs will not be addressed. PIE workers, reflective and resilient, accept the use of substances is answering a deep need in the person, and will look for creative ways to engage them as they self-medicate, such as impromptu moments of connection.

The care home is in this instance an excellent environment to form rudimentary bonds with such individuals. With 24-hour access to staff they can return to the home at any time and find someone to talk to, there is no specific appointment times to miss, no letters saying they have failed because they didn't turn up. So, whilst the care environment certainly brings with it its own set of problems regarding power imbalance in relationship making and being part of a much hated 'system', the continuity of care provided by the home cannot be replicated by any health or drug and alcohol service. Some of the best work in laying the foundations of future acceptance has been done by night staff who have proved to the chaotic resident that there is a trustable entity available to them when it suits *them* and not the service.

> *Colin came to the home as a 40-year-old struggling with debt to the local council and dealers; he was in a vulnerable position and about to lose his tenancy and faced violent retribution for the money he owed on the streets. His drug use had risen sharply and he was displaying symptoms of his schizophrenia – talking to his voices, hitting himself in the face – despite claiming he was ok.*
>
> *Colin accepted the placement at the home but did not engage with staff. He spent a lot of time out of the home having found a new supplier of heroin and Spice, and the times he was in the home were largely spent in drug-induced unconsciousness.*
>
> *Staff tried to find ways to connect with Colin but to little avail – he refused one-to-one support and didn't enjoy being around other people. He didn't like to show 'weakness' in the face of his illness and attempted to control his symptoms by isolating himself and heavy drug use.*
>
> *After a month of little meaningful engagement Colin began to come into the staff office late at night sometimes for some biscuits and, over time, a chat with one of the night staff. This became a habit – he obviously felt comfortable being up at night and with fewer people around.*
>
> *This regular chat with the night staff gave Colin confidence in the home and proved staff to be non-judgemental in their support of him. The unconditional positive regard shown to him reduced the sense of persecution and labelling he clearly felt and hated. The night staff fed back to the day team about his wellbeing and mental state.*
>
> *Over time Colin began to access day staff as well, tentatively building the first steps of a relationship with them. With the acceptance he felt, his drug use reduced slightly, giving the staff a chance to better assess and support his mental health needs and to build connections.*

40 *Relationships*

>   *One day Colin sat down and asked to speak to a mental health professional with a staff member present. In the meeting he discussed openly and thoroughly the difficulties he was having with his voices and how he'd like to change his anti-psychotic medication, which was agreed. He also accessed the drug and alcohol service and became stable on a buprenorphine script.*
>
>   *The building of rapport with Colin by the night staff led to him accessing services he hadn't used for years and contributed to him leading a much more stable, well, and fulfilling existence. The 24-hour staffing of the home provided an 'always on' approach to creating points of connection with such a chaotic individual with very positive results.*

The negative effects of the drugs the residents use to moderate their emotional landscape invariably means they are unable to sustain living the isolated existence they have spent years creating. Along with the offer of unconditional support comes the feeling of being trapped by circumstance and confusion by the caring signals they are receiving from the workers. They will feel overwhelmed, tired, and often full of shame. A slow but sure approach to creating a healthy relationship will help to mitigate this.

Knowledge of the Self-Medication Hypothesis leads workers away from seeing substance use as criminal behaviour and shows it to be a process of self-regulation – there should be focus not on the pleasure or reward aspects of drug use but on the distress relief. Addictions develop in environmental context – social, genetic, psychological, and biological[15] – and will therefore need a complex response if we are to work successfully with it. The PIE care home, catering for social, physical, and emotional aspects of the resident, has the potential to be an integral part of the answer.

Pre-treatment and creating a common language

When building relationships, the words we use and how we use them are important: they frame the purpose and aspirations of the relationship builders and give a sense of direction to the alliance. Language can be playful, functional, dismissive, or supportive and used wisely help balance the needs of the person with the needs of the service. Narrative therapists Friedman and Combs state: 'speaking isn't neutral or passive. Every time we speak, we bring forth a reality. Each time we share words, we give legitimacy to the distinctions that these words bring forth.'[16] Thus psychiatrists, doctors, and other health professionals (including carers) use clinical terminology which creates, intentionally or otherwise, a framework for the professional/

patient dynamic. With this in mind it is clear why workers with trauma and in institutions must be mindful, that is, psychologically informed, as to their choice of language and the effect it may have upon the client.

Within the care home there are, naturally, words and phrases that assist the workers to run a safe and successful environment – meds run, welfare check, risk assessment, and so on – that are seemingly innocuous, however they place the resident in the role of 'patient'. Working in a PIE care home asks us to reduce the impact of these structural phrases to a minimum whilst deliberately co-creating a shared language between residents and workers that promotes equality.

Adults living in social care will have worked their way through many relationships with various professionals, all having had one common denominator; that it is they who have been asked to speak the language of the other. The words the clients use in response to this professional, powerful language can often be dismissive and volatile, or overly passive. This is a verbal ping-pong based on mistrust.

Phrases like these are common:

> *'Yap, yap, yap, that's all they do.'*
> *'They say I'm schizophrenic [throws up hands] but I don't bloody know!'*
> *'She [the psychiatrist] says I have to, but I don't know if I want to.'*
> *'I'm not going [to the meeting], I'm not a fucking fraggle!'*

Not only do these phrases exude a lack of control, they do not chime with the values of person-centred care.

After years as revolving door patients our residents have become inured to the language of recovery; it has become a worn-out set of tropes and has lost its efficacy. Chronic service users, having long given up on the real meaning of this language, begin to use it as currency to meet their own ends – often a misplaced desire to be left alone to cope as best they can. This is also true for mental health diagnoses – they can become as tedious as an unwanted day job, traded upon to keep the professional patient in a sort of stasis – neither in crisis nor becoming well. This tired pattern – represented by phrases like: 'I'm going to get myself clean, I'll go to the drug agency tomorrow' – can in turn affect the un-reflective worker, creating a despondent, disaffected cycle where real, genuine, belief in the residents' ability to change fades ('Oh it's just Mark, same old, same old, says he's going to stop using, I'll believe it when I see it, he'll never change').

I once attended a multi-disciplinary meeting with a resident, who at 32 was stable and competent in terms of living skills, and was being asked to start looking at the next phase of accommodation by social services.

He'd also begun to say that he was finding the 24-hour care environment restrictive and that he wanted more freedom to live as he wanted. As the conversation progressed it became clear that he was going to be offered council accommodation, and due to his general wellbeing and life skills would have little community support. At this he began to say he wasn't well enough, that his schizophrenic symptoms were too severe for him to cope. He asked for a halfway house which would give him the freedom of his own tenancy with the support of in-house workers for day-to-day housekeeping.

It was clear that he was dependent on his symptoms to broker a support package despite showing few signs that they were causing him any distress. I asked him if he had to remain unwell enough to access support and benefits but also wanted to be well enough to live a free and happy life. He laughed and replied: 'Yes, that's it.'

This resident's use of diagnoses and mental health symptoms to negotiate a deal with social services shows the incongruence that long-term service users can experience within themselves, needing to promote themselves as unwell whilst wanting to stop the symptoms of their illness. The acceptance and use of 'unwellness', which is a damaging identity, can lead to a lifetime of low self-esteem and lack of purpose.

I believe long-term service users are at least as, if not more, difficult to truly engage than any other group of people – they have been through the first cycle of using the positive words of recovery and with (possibly multiple) relapse have lost belief in their power. Without real human connection giving energy to the prospect of recovery, the words become at best ineffective, at worst damaging.

Narrative therapy aims to free the worker from using clinical language and gives voice to the clients' own language. By moving focus away from labels, stereotypes, and diagnosis, a space is created to highlight people's talents and strengths; this in turn shifts the narrative away from the client as a professional patient and towards that of a 'whole' person. Narrative therapy lends weight to the PIE ideology of putting relationships at the heart of the process and that change is always possible. The approach asks workers to look for 'sparkling moments' – moments or conversations which move away from the narrative of a problem-saturated life, and leads client and worker towards a strengths-based narrative. Narrative therapy has been used by J. Levy in the creation of pre-treatment pathways for hard-to-reach clients. Born from working with the street homeless in Canada pre-treatment is, much like the PIE concept, transferable to other human services settings.

Levy's pre-treatment principles provide a framework, separated into five areas much like the PIE approach. They are:

1 Enhance safety – Stabilise acute symptoms and utilise opportunity for further work
2 Relationship formation – Attempt to engage in a manner that promotes trust, safety, and autonomy
3 Develop common language – Attempt to understand a person's world by learning the meaning of his or her gestures, words, and actions by promoting mutual understanding and well-defined goals
4 Promote and support change – Achieve and maintain change by exploring ambivalence, reinforcing healthy behaviours, and developing skills
5 Cultural and ecological effects – Prepare clients for successful adaption to new relationships, services, and resources[17]

It can be used successfully to engage disaffected professional patients and involves finding a common language between the worker and client that can invigorate and feels authentic.

The case study of David, earlier in this chapter, shows these principles in action. First, we saw his more extreme behaviour as a form of communication and ensured he remained safe, we created consistent fair boundaries, and used clear, accessible language to support him as he changed his behaviour. The goals we set were reasonable and he was helped to accept and then achieve them. The support he was given allowed him to access other services such as the hospital and GP.

A shared language comes from a common framework or experience – it relates to the real world. Care homes are an ideal environment for workers and clients to create a shared language of recovery. To achieve best outcomes a resident must feel invested in their life script – recovery needs a sense of safety, trust, and self-agency[18] – and carers can provide this secure base. By mindfully reducing the use of clinical language staff can re-humanise the residents' experience, giving them support not as clinicians but as a professional family.

The importance of using language thoughtfully and of being mindful when building relationships when caring for the traumatised and mentally ill is captured well here:

> The spiritual disease of the long-term mentally ill can only be understood if we put aside our technical language and speak in human terms . . . Today, we will put aside the word treatment, and instead talk of healing . . . we will not speak of counselling, but rather of consoling; we will not speak of illness, but rather of woundedness.[19]

The PIE care home worker has a unique chance to support the resident as they begin to heal.

This chapter has reflected KLOE:

S1

- 'The service is particularly creative in the ways it involves and works with people to understand their diverse circumstances and individual needs.'
- 'Staff develop positive and trusting relationships with people that help to keep them safe; staff have the time they need to do so, or make the time.'

S2

- 'Staff show empathy and have an enabling attitude that encourages people to challenge themselves, while recognising and respecting their lifestyle choice.'

E1

- 'There is a truly holistic approach to assessing, planning and delivering care and support.'

C1

- 'There is a strong, visible person-centred culture . . . Staff demonstrate a real empathy for the people they care for.'
- 'The service anticipates people's needs and recognises distress and discomfort at the earliest stage. It offers respectful and supportive care.'

W1

- 'The service's vision and values are imaginative and people are at the heart of the service.'

W3

- 'The service finds innovative and creative ways to enable people to be empowered and voice their opinions.'

Notes

1 Sourced from www.cqc.org.uk/sites/default/files/new_reports/INS2–5964836491.pdf
2 Rogers, C. R., *On Becoming a Person* (Constable, 2004), 34.

3 Herman, J., *Trauma and Recovery* (Basic Books, 1997), 135.
4 Khantzian, E. and Albanese, M., *Understanding Addiction as Self Medication* (Good Time Books, 2013), 69.
5 Evans, A. and Coccoma, P., *Trauma-informed Care: How Neuroscience Influences Practice* (Routledge 2016), 44.
6 Herman, *Trauma and Recovery*, 104.
7 Herman, *Trauma and Recovery*, 111.
8 Evans and Coccoma, *Trauma-informed Care*, 32.
9 LeDoux, 2000; van der Kolk, 2006; Evans and Coccoma, *Trauma-informed Care*, 29.
10 Cockersell, P. (Ed.), *Social Exclusion, Compound Trauma and Recovery* (Jessica Kingsley Publishers, 2018), 71.
11 Herman, *Trauma and Recovery*, 56.
12 Levy, J. S. (Ed.) with Johnson, R., *Cross-Cultural Dialogues on Homelessness: From Pretreatment Strategies to Psychologically Informed Environments* (Loving Healing Press, 2017), 57.
13 Sourced from www.bma.org.uk/advice/work-life-support/your-wellbeing/vicarious-trauma
14 Cockersell, *Social Exclusion, Compound Trauma and Recovery*, 112.
15 Khanzian, E. and Albanese, M., *Understanding Addiction as Self-Medication* (Good Time Books, 2013), 31.
16 Friedman and Combs, *Narrative Therapy: The Social Construction of Preferred Realities* (Norton, 1996), 29, 58.
17 Levy with Johnson, *Cross-Cultural Dialogues on Homelessness*, Appendix Table 1.
18 Castillo, H., *The Reality of Recovery in Personality Disorder* (London: Jessica Kingsley Publishers, 2016); Cockersell, *Social Exclusion, Compound Trauma and Recovery*, 112.
19 Deegan, P., 1986; Levy with Johnson, *Cross-Cultural Dialogues on Homelessness*, 61.

5 Reflective practice

In this chapter we will:

- Explore reflective practice as a key area of the PIE approach
- Be introduced to Gibbs' six stage reflective cycle
- See how reflective practice can be used to work with aggression
- See reflective practice as a tool to reduce bias
- Use case studies to show real-world examples of reflective practice

Using reflective practice is an integral part of the PIE initiative and, along with building relationships, is a binding force of the model. Together they are the foundation upon which the five key elements are built. Reflective practice promotes workers to learn from their experience, and for the team to better their collective work practice. We can use reflective practice throughout our working day, individually or in groups, as well as in more formal supervisions and meetings.

As they attempt to negotiate life, survivors of trauma, caught in a whirlwind of addiction and complex behaviours, can seem unduly aggressive and confusingly erratic. To workers, this behaviour can be disorientating and discomforting, seemingly without purpose and yet hugely self-injurious. Trauma is contagious,[1] and we must use all the tools at our disposal to accept and counteract this – reflexive responses to an already complicated situation will only compound residents' fears, paranoia, and feelings of isolation. Working with complex needs means we are at risk of misunderstanding the meaning behind challenging behaviour, or missing the cues for support being given, as they become jumbled up with the day-to-day activity around the home. Organising planned time to stop and reflect helps workers to unpick positive narrative threads which will help them improve their care giving.

For workers to support residents holistically they must be prepared to reflect on both the residents' history and also their own life experience. Building trusting relationships is a joint venture and one which will inevitably prove difficult at times. Gaining different perspectives through group reflection gives workers the chance to see situations from various angles, and to adapt their way of working accordingly.

This chapter explores use of reflective practice in the PIE care home, using case studies to demonstrate its efficacy.

What is reflective practice?

Reflective practice is a chance to evaluate and learn from a situation. Lucas argues it involves a systematic enquiry to improve and deepen our understanding of practice[2] – that is, it is a deliberate and organised action. So, whilst we may reflect in passing on our actions throughout the day, there should also be time made for structured reflective time. In a PIE, as we increase focus upon the emotional interactions between workers and clients, and on workers embodying safe boundaries, workers will need space and support to consider how their actions are affecting residents, and vice versa.

The 2012 *Good Practice Guide* explains reflective practice as:

> the process of recapturing and analysing actions and processes in order to learn from incidents and improve responsiveness of the service. It enables clients to feel that their problems are recognised and that they are being heard. It gives staff a perspective on the emotional challenges of their work.[3]

Liz, a domestic worker, is feeling very frustrated with John, a resident. At lunchtime he's moved from seat to seat in the dining room with his plate, dropping food on the floor and scattering it across tables. He's quite drunk and a stroke has left him with limited use on one side. This is a regular occurrence and Liz is beginning to get irate with him. She comes into the office and throws her hands up into the air, saying:–

'I've had enough of it! He's doing it again! He's doing it just to annoy me!'

We reflect upon the situation. Liz feels that John is targeting her in his behaviour and is deliberately messing up the dining room. When she tells him to sit in one place he gets up and moves.

Throughout the conversation we realise that a lot of Liz's frustration comes from the fact her shift finishes just after lunchtime. Throughout the rest of the day she is diligent in her duties, but by midday is becoming tired and doesn't want to have to re-clean the whole dining room. We also reflect on use of language and agree that asking, not telling, would be a better, more compassionate, way to approach John.

We consider that John has lost a lot of his independence over the last few years; prior to his stroke he was a well-known street drinker, an active part of the street community.

With this in mind we can see John's behaviour as a symptom of his own frustration about where life has taken him – these small acts of rebellion signify a greater sense of loss of control over his life.

Later, in a staff meeting, we reflect as a group on how to support both John and Liz. We realise that Liz needs to feel supported and that John needs to feel some sense of power.

We decide that John should be prompted to use one place at lunchtime and that care staff would sit and engage him to help this, but he could move around however he so wished, and that care staff would clean up after John – allaying Liz's frustration, and helping her relax.

A few days later I hear Liz and John in the dining room:

'Can you please not move around John, I don't want to have to tidy up again, I'm tired.'

'Yes, love, no problem, no problem at all.'

Without pausing for a moment, and helping Liz take a step back, the situation would, to her, have remained solely John's fault, which was not a fair perspective. Through the reflective process, and with support from care staff, Liz became more relaxed and was more thoughtful about her language towards John, who in turn responded to her calmly.

Gibbs' reflective cycle

There are a number of models to support reflective practice – one of the most used is Gibbs'. His six-step reflective cycle emphasises learning from experiences, which suits the care environment. Each of the six stages uses questions as prompts which makes the model easy to use in practice. The stages are:[4]

Stage	Key Question
Description	What happened?
Feelings	What were you thinking and feeling?
Evaluation	Was the experience good or bad?
Analysis	What sense can you make out of the situation?
Conclusion	What else could you have done?
Action plan	If it arose again what would you do?

Particularly useful are stage two and four of the cycle – 'feelings' and 'analysis'. As workers move away from a task-based environment, and towards a more holistic, psychologically aware one, their understanding of what success means will necessarily change, as will their relationships with residents. Accepting and reflecting upon their emotional responses to residents and situations will improve congruence, and better authentic connections around the home.

This process requires workers to think about their actions and behaviour at a deeper level, and to become more critically reflective. The team dynamic will change as they are promoted to become critical friends and to explore improving the group dynamic between workers and residents.

The reflective cycle can also be a protective device as staff create trusting relationships with residents.

Helen is feeling deeply hurt by Tasha. She has been Tasha's keyworker for some time and they have a strong relationship. They often go into town shopping together and go out for cups of coffee regularly. The relationship feels natural, and has become trusting.

After a trip out, Helen comes into the office and puts her bag away. She realises £30 has gone missing from her purse. It becomes clear that Tasha must have taken it when Helen went to the toilet in a café and left her bag on the chair.

We could use the reflective cycle to help Helen as she worked through the situation.

Description – what happened? They were having a chat in their favourite café as usual. Helen nipped to the toilet, leaving her bag on the chair without thinking about it. There was no sign from the way Tasha behaved on her return that anything was different or remiss. Returning to the home she found money missing, but at first she didn't want to mention it as she felt awkward about the mistake.

Feelings – what were you thinking and feeling? Helen felt a mixture of many feelings. Anger at herself for leaving the bag in the café, anger with Tasha for stealing from her. Embarrassment that as a professional worker she had made a mistake. Frustration that Tasha, who seemed to be doing 'well', would do something like that. Hurt that Tasha would put money above their relationship which had been so carefully cultivated. Worry for Tasha's future at the home.

Evaluation – what was good and bad about the experience? That Helen felt so comfortable with Tasha was a positive, that she left her bag shows a sense of trust had been fostered. The negative was for Helen to be stolen from and to feel so hurt by Tasha's actions.

Analysis – what sense can I make of the situation? Helen recognised that to feel hurt was completely natural, and that her embarrassment proved she cared about her job and took it very seriously. She could see that her feelings of frustration meant she had built a good bond with Tasha which demonstrated commitment. Her feelings of anger were perfectly natural – her privacy had been violated by somebody going through her private belongings. Helen recognised that Tasha's actions weren't aimed at her, but opportunistic, and as a drug user, her addiction would sadly take precedence over any relationship as she self-medicated her feelings of rage and anxiety.

Conclusion – what else could I have done? In the future Helen would keep her bag with her at all times. As a team we could use the story to underline the importance of keeping personal items safe, and to remember that addicted residents would have urges which could drive anti-social or self-destructive behaviour.

Action plan – if it arose again what would I do? Helen would remember that her emotional response showed commitment and dedication to her work. She would try to feel confident to talk about any similar events openly, seeing that this could help other staff learn.

In this case, after the reflective process and much conversation within the team, it was decided that if Tasha showed signs of being sorry and paid the money back that no further action would be taken, which she did. The relationship between Helen and Tasha remained positive, our actions proved to Tasha that making mistakes did not automatically mean eviction and abandonment. The staff team also learnt a valuable lesson from the situation about remaining vigilant around personal possessions.

Working with aggression

The reflective cycle helps us to work with anti-social and aggressive behaviour. After moments of stress or heightened emotions it is good practice to reflect on the situation. Taking time to do this will reduce the chance of compassion fatigue or trauma. Ghaye writes: 'maybe reflective practices offer us a way of trying to make sense of the uncertainty in our workplaces and the courage to work competently and ethically at the edge of order and chaos'.[5]

Creating time to reflect on untoward events not only helps the workers involved to not take work home or over-ruminate on a situation, but is a valuable tool to help less experienced staff members 'learn the ropes'. Bassot writes: 'students often marvel at the knowledge of experienced practitioners when they observe them on placements', but 'these practitioners often cannot explain how they know things'. She goes on to use an analogy of learning to drive – that when we can, 'we might be fooled into thinking we could do this all along'.[6]

Reflective practice helps the whole team develop and improve their response to challenging situations, and helps to keep everybody (service user, peers, and workers) safe. Bourne writes: 'it is important that whenever we work with someone who may be potentially dangerous, we must not do so in isolation . . . To work in a group we need opportunities to continually reflect particularly on:

- The interpersonal dynamics operating between us and the service user
- How we are working with them and how this is similar or different to work with other service users
- Areas that we may be avoiding or being caught up in
- How we can make sense of the service user's behaviour, and whether alternative explanations are being prematurely dismissed.'[7]

Al is an imposing man, and at around 6' 4" he towers over most of the staff and can become very physically dominant. He has few boundaries and is furious with 'the NHS' for forcing him, as he sees it, to take anti-psychotic medication. He places Highwater House into the category of 'NHS', even though we have little to do with his medication regime.

Some staff enjoy working with Al, they feel quite comfortable around him, and feel they can 'handle' him. Other staff, who bear the brunt of his aggression, are finding him increasingly confrontational, with one member of staff beginning to dread coming to work.

One evening Al had become so angry that he slammed his door until the frame had come away from the wall, and he had trashed his room. The next day he was calmer, but not capitulatory.

In individual and group reflective sessions we discussed Al's situation. Some staff argued for him staying at Highwater, some argued he was too intimidating and was making the service unsafe and unsettled, not least for other residents.

Through the reflective process we concluded that it was Al's voice that should be heard. He didn't want to live at Highwater House – he saw it as a restrictive and coercive environment, which was driving his challenging behaviour. All of the staff's arguments for and against his staying were personal views largely based on their personal successes or failures with Al.

Al was referred on from the service, and his behaviour calmed down considerably.

Al's case gave the team the opportunity to reflect on their personal dynamics with residents. Working with challenging behaviour can give workers a sense of pride, but this should not be to the detriment of other team mates.

Al had become a 'special case' where he was being treated with kid gloves to ameliorate the worst of his aggression, however, upon reflection, this approach was never going to be sustainable as he didn't want to be in the service.

The reflective process allowed staff to pause and step outside the 'just cope' mindset they had collectively fallen into. Al's voice could then be heard and we could 'make sense of the service user's behaviour' – he simply did not want to live at Highwater House and was trying to communicate this.

Bias and roles

Reflective practice can be used to challenge bias and discrimination. Accepting that we are a product of our upbringing and past experiences, it is inevitable that workers will bring subconscious bias into the workplace. This might, for example, involve cultural or social prejudice, ageism, sexism, or strong feelings about drug use. We are all affected by our surroundings, the views in the media, and within our team. Working with vulnerable clients, who have little agency over their environment, means workers must be especially careful not to compound any previous experiences of intolerance or discrimination. We must reflect on our behaviour and responses to residents and ask ourselves to challenge any preconceived ideas of how or why people might be behaving in a particular way.

> 'Oh, it's just Adam, he's a drinker – he goes off like a bottle of pop, just like they all do!'
> 'Watch out, Keith's showing signs of hearing things, and schizophrenics can be dangerous.'
> 'Why doesn't he just stop taking heroin? It's a dirty drug.'
> 'I bet he has to steal to get his fix.'
> 'They're all the same, they say they'll go to the meeting but. . . .'

In traditional care settings the roles of staff and residents are strictly defined and separated. This separation leads to a 'lumping together' of the resident population and so, accidental, stigmatisation. Staff might therefore discuss 'the residents' or use 'they' – 'oh, they like to go on activities', for example. This in turn, subconsciously or otherwise, creates a faceless, and therefore institutionalised, feel to care provision.

Reflective practice helps to avoid treating clients as a homogenous group, asking us to consider everyone as individuals – and challenging the worker to look beyond stereotypes.

It is through training that workers gain knowledge, but through reflective practice that they use it.

Reflective practice in a care home

A key factor to using the PIE principles in a care home is to recognise that systemic care can be an abrasive and debilitating experience for the service user, especially when the care environment is lumped in with other psychiatric or containing settings into one amorphous 'system'.

Reflective practice gives staff the opportunity to step back from their (probably quite correct) belief that they are providing good care and to see the service through the eyes of the traumatised client. Are the routines of the home causing a feeling of coercion in the resident? Certainly, residents who have been through the mental health system will have experienced, personally or vicariously, physical restraint and compulsion to medicate. They may feel the care home's habitual patterns to be a similar invasive force, or trigger memories of a more punitive environment.

To work successfully with complex needs, workers *have* to consider different perspectives to situations, and recognise that the more complex the problems, the more nuanced the responses need to be. We should reflect upon the power imbalances within the home – are they creating feelings of shame in the resident, and thus causing certain behaviour? Are the residents' self-destructive behaviours symbolic reenactments of abuse?[8] Are we medicalising mental distress which is actually the perfectly natural social and behavioural response of a person 'placed' in care for the first time? And, as we welcome residents into the community of the home, we must accept that their feelings of success may not marry with ours – or may not follow the expected, prescribed recovery process. Maté writes: 'even in cases where abstinence is not achieved, redemption would mean the reintegration of the user into the larger community and the restoration of his values as a person in his own eyes'.[9] We should reflect upon our own hopes for people, and strive to recognise that our hopes will not be theirs.

We can use the reflective process to soften the edges of the system, and to create a suspension of disbelief where there is power equity between workers and residents. In this way we create a benign group dynamic – one where every member is accepted as an individual, with a valued personal story. Healing takes place in groups: 'the restoration of social bonds begins with the discovery that one is not alone',[10] and reflective practice is a key tool in the PIE worker's toolkit to ensure clients feel welcome and accepted.

> This chapter has reflected KLOE:
>
> S6
>
> - 'Learning is based on a thorough analysis and investigation of things that go wrong.'
>
> E2
>
> - 'Staff training is developed and delivered around individual needs.'
>
> C1
>
> - 'There is a strong, visible person-centred culture.'
>
> R1
>
> - 'Staff have opportunities for learning, development, and reflective practice on equality and diversity.'

Notes

1. Herman, J., *Trauma and Recovery* (Basic Books, 1997), 140.
2. Lucas, P., (1991) Reflection, new practices and the need for flexibility in supervising student teachers. *Journal of Further and Higher Education*, 15 (2), 84–93; Bassot, B., *The Reflective Practice Guide* (Routledge, 2016), 1.
3. https://eprints.soton.ac.uk/340022/1/Good%2520practice%2520guide%2520-%2520%2520Psychologically%2520informed%2520services%2520for%2520homeless%2520people%2520.pdf, 6.
4. Sourced from www.ed.ac.uk/reflection/reflectors-toolkit/reflecting-on-experience/gibbs-reflective-cycle
5. Ghaye, 2000, 7, sourced from www.open.ac.uk/opencetl/sites/www.open.ac.uk.opencetl/files/files/ecms/web-content/Finlay-(2008)-Reflecting-on-reflective-practice-PBPL-paper-52.pdf
6. Bassot, *The Reflective Practice Guide*, 4 and 10.
7. Bourne, I., *Facing Danger in the Helping Professions* (Open University Press, 2013), 160.
8. Herman, *Trauma and Recovery*, 166.
9. Maté, G., *In the Realm of the Hungry Ghosts* (Vermillion, 2018), 295.
10. Herman, *Trauma and Recovery*, 215.

6 Elastic tolerance

In this chapter we will:

- Discover elastic tolerance as an effective and creative process of behaviour management
- Discover how to separate the service user from the problem, and to humanise the worker
- See that the care system can cause distress
- Find that explaining our actions helps residents to understand our reasons
- Ask staff to embody safe boundaries, not to instil rules

> Elastic – 'able to encompass much variety and change; flexible and adaptable.'
> Also – 'able to resume its normal shape spontaneously after being stretched or compressed' – i.e. we collectively return to the baseline without attributing blame after reflection and explanation.
> Tolerance – 'The ability or willingness to tolerate the existence of opinions or behaviour that one dislikes or disagrees with.'[1]

In this chapter we are introduced to elastic tolerance, that is, to work creatively with anti-social or 'difficult' behaviour, or behaviour we may not agree with ourselves. Our aim is to support the resident to self-regulate their impulsive or destructive actions, and for them to choose to work positively within the home's ecology. This idea is not new. Charles Dickens, in his book *American Notes*, describes the superintendent of a hospital sitting down to dinner with patients: 'moral influence alone restrains the more violent', and that therefore restricting devices could be reduced.[2] In his study of therapeutic communities, *Community as Doctor*, Robert Rapoport uses the term 'elastic boundaries' explained as: 'flexible enough to provide rationales for various courses of action'.[3] A key aspect of elastic tolerance is to always explain why any action is being taken.

Our ambition is to avoid isolating or evicting the resident or of increasing feelings of abandonment in them. We are aiming to halt the destructive cycle that revolving door clients are often caught up in: low-level disruption and aggression; a refusal to play a role in the wellbeing of the community; defiant outbursts; and habitual patterns of challenging behaviour. For the resident, common outcomes of this cycle are feelings of distress and abandonment and a subdued and fearful expectation that they will be 'punished' for this often-compulsive behaviour. This cycle feeds a narrative of 'deserved isolation' and unlovability, reaffirming and exacerbating the trauma they have previously experienced. Many residents over the years, when they have moved in to the home, have said to us: 'Don't worry, I'll behave' – a childlike phrase, and one of submission. Indeed, it brings to mind how a prisoner might speak to an officer at the beginning of a custodial sentence rather than to a carer at the start of a journey towards stability and recovery. We should be mindful of how our environment might impact a new resident, their past experiences of 'locked' institutions and patterns of behaviour born from years of having little power in their lives.

We will see that working with their behaviours by using our relationships and the environment mindfully, rather than simply imposing punitive measures (The Rules), leads service users, with the help of their peer group and staff, to willingly alter their behaviour.

This style of behavioural management reflects the Care Act's key principles of *Proportionality* – that is, to ensure the least intrusive response to the risk presented – and *Protection* – to support and represent those in need.

Placing such importance on the staff's duty to respond to challenging behaviours mindfully also supports the CQC Key Line of Enquiry – Safe. This area ensures people are free from abuse, including institutional, mental, or psychological abuse. The emphasis that using elastic tolerance places upon staff to consider and respond creatively exemplifies person-centred support. The consistent reflective practice amongst team mates – both ad hoc and in team meetings – around how to best positively support a challenging resident ensures lessons are learnt in a timely and constructive manner.

To work positively with challenging behaviour requires us to accept two premises: that, as we have explored in the chapter on trauma-informed practice, behaviour has meaning, is a form of communication, and is driven by past experiences or feelings; and, second, that the client is ultimately searching for balance – homeostasis – but is blocking or being blocked in some way from achieving this state of wellbeing. Using these as our foundation for behaviour management within the home ensures we are consistently responding reflectively and empathically. If we are to successfully support in-need people we must move beyond simply 'telling them the rules', we must humanise the process.

> A great deal of aggression towards us as professionals has very little to do with us personally – they are angry with the system, with authority, with their situation – it's just that we happen to represent all those things right now.[4]

As we explore working creatively with anti-social behaviour, we will see how reducing punitive measures, increasing positive reinforcement, and giving reason for our actions helps the resident to self-regulate their emotions and behaviour. With this support they will begin to mentalise and to question their own actions. The PIE framework assists the worker to use themselves as a prosocial tool by embodying acceptable, suitable social boundaries in a supported environment.

Every decision we make around behaviour management should reflect one key question – 'Are we keeping this person as safe as we can?'. In supervision, when asked to clarify a grey area about rules in the home, this is my response: Are your actions designed to keep that person, above all, safe?

The message of this chapter also reflects NICE guideline NG10 (2015) which offers recommendations around short-term management of violence and aggression. This guideline states, under the general principles of de-escalation, workers should:

> Establish a close working relationship with service users at the earliest opportunity and sensitively monitor changes in their mood or composure that may lead to aggression or violence.
>
> Use a wide range of verbal and non-verbal skills and interactional techniques to avoid or manage known 'flashpoint' situations (such as refusing a service user's request, asking them to stop doing something they wish to do or asking that they do something they don't wish to do) without provoking aggression.
>
> Communicate respect for and empathy with the service user at all stages of de-escalation.[5]

In a PIE, placing trusting relationships at the forefront of every interaction and improving our psychological awareness, we are following these guidelines and ensuring we provide a better service for our traumatised clients. The bonds forged means that in a moment of anger the resident will be less likely to depersonalise the worker and attack them as a 'faceless' point of authority; rather, it becomes an opportunity to depersonalise the *issue*, that is, to see the behaviour as distinct from the resident, and work together to find a suitable solution. The problem is the problem, the person is not the problem.[6]

Breaking the trauma cycle and recognising risk

PIE workers have a duty to learn the language of trauma and survivor behaviour. As we explored in the chapter on building relationships, how we respond to 'difficult' behaviour (such as David's) will have huge ramifications for the residents' wellbeing.

We know that response to trauma can create dramatic somatic and emotional responses in survivors which might seem erratic or 'unacceptable' to others; however, as PIE workers our validation of their experience is key to enacting positive change. Trauma can cause a loss of a sense of self, hopelessness for the future, hypervigilance and mistrust, irritability and self-destructive or risky behaviour.[7] Sadly, these expressions of trauma often lead to further isolation, and compound previous traumatic experiences; it is the worst sort of vicious cycle. The person is caught in a perpetual self-destructive vortex, constantly reaffirming that they are not worthy of help or support, and excluding them from helping services (whose inclusion criteria for helping is often no history of violence, no aggression, and so on). This is our typical revolving door client.

Before a resident has even moved in to a service, staff are pre-determining how they will respond to the client using risk assessments. They therefore arrive with the weight of years of risk, catalogued and organised by various services, upon their shoulders. This stack of negative paperwork pre-empts a negative partnership between client and worker, and whilst risk assessments are an inevitability, we should strive to work with the person and not their risk. Imagine applying for a job and before going to the interview someone sending a list of your worst actions, your most erratic moments to the interviewers; would this make you comfortable? Would you feel fairly considered for the post?

Service users are inevitably defined by their worst actions, their most aggressive act, and risk assessments do not allow for mitigating factors; the human story that surrounds the risk event. We should remain aware that risk is at least partly a subjective phenomenon; it involves a worker's interpretation of events. We must strive to stay aware of, and reflect upon, our filters and prejudices, and stop ourselves from stereotyping or stigmatising already vulnerable people. Doing so helps us balance risk with need and care. In this way the service user can start their placement with as little negative bias as possible, allowing them to greet their new home and workers as the person they would like to be, not just the one they have been.

> Stu came to Highwater House as a well-known street drinker renowned for his aggressive attitude and willingness to fight. He was known to 'get in people's faces' and, in his mid-forties, had spent the majority of his adult life in and out of various institutions and prisons. He was proud of the teardrop tattooed under his eye – a symbol of long prison sentences and proof of his capacity to be violent.
>
> We were warned that Stu was 'trouble', 'difficult', and told we'd 'have our work cut out with that one'. A local health centre worker laughed when she heard he was moving in and just said 'Good luck!' He was framed by every service we spoke to as high risk, explosive and unreachable, that it would be a waste of time trying to work with him and that he was more trouble than he was worth.
>
> This wholly negative image of Stu – full of risk and aggression – was also well used by Stu himself as a carapace to keep himself safe; with his reputation preceding him he was largely protected from many of the difficulties that street and institutionalised living brings.
>
> Stu's first weeks at the home were inevitably difficult for him and, at times, the staff. He regularly challenged the boundaries at the home, determinedly promoting himself as untouchable – he raised his voice, swore, clenched his fists, threatened violence, and stared staff down. He'd point to his teardrop tattoo – a gesture he clearly felt protected by as it symbolised his violent past.
>
> Staff did not allow this show of bravado to intimidate them, and focussed on building rapport with Stu. That they were unflustered by these almost theatrical shows of force left Stu confused – his role of aggressor was not placing staff into the role of victim as it should. In fact this behaviour was being responded to with kindness and he, but not his behaviour, was being consistently told that he was welcome at the home.
>
> As the weeks passed, Stu's behaviour changed; as he felt increasingly settled at the home and accepted it as a non-threatening, benign environment, he became less volatile. The anti-social, aggressive behaviour that had provided a quick route to safety on the streets and in prison held little purpose in the caring environment. It seemed like a relief when he began to drop such a tiring façade.
>
> Over the time Stu spent with us he went through a remarkable transformation from an 'aggressive drinker' and 'violent repeat offender' to that of a middle-aged introspective charming man. As he reduced his use of alcohol, a key driver to his previous behaviour, it became clear

he suffered from acute anxiety which he had been self-medicating with the alcohol. Within the security of the home he experimented with sobriety and prescribed medication, eventually becoming stable enough to move on to his own accommodation.

In Stu's story we can see how he used aggressive behaviour as a tool to keep himself safe, but that the troubling outcome was that he had become, through risk assessments and the way he engaged with services, known solely as that aggressive character. The negative behaviours he used so well to ensure his security had become an all-encompassing explanation of him, leaving little room for other sides to be revealed. He was, deliberately and incidentally, placed in a negative role which people then responded to. It was by separating the behaviour from the man, and by staff subverting the role play, that created the time and space necessary for him to begin the process of becoming a more balanced human being.

Projection

As PIE workers we accept the traumatised resident projecting their frustrations and fears onto us and the environment, and see this process as an opportunity to instil fair and consistent boundaries – clear, understood, and, importantly, reinforced through the worker's own behaviour and actions. It is in this difficult area of supporting damaged people that we can use our improved understanding of psychological theory and practice that becoming a PIE brings to protect ourselves from compassion fatigue. Remember, the PIE framework supports the worker by providing reason for what may seem very unreasonable behaviour.

> *'You fat bitch!'*
> *This insult seemingly comes out of nowhere, and for no reason. Mary, a resident, is standing in the foyer and has turned on Michelle, a project worker.*
> *'You disgust me. Look at you, you're pathetic. Think you're something special, don't you? Well you're not, you're nothing, nobody.'*
> *Michelle comes into the office, visibly upset. 'She just called me a fat bitch, who does she think she is? She can't do that, she's so horrible!'*
> *Michelle has always been kind to Mary, an individual who has experienced severe trauma involving neglect and physical and sexual abuse throughout her childhood. She self-medicates with alcohol every day and will often become extremely verbally aggressive.*
> *We talk the situation over, and agree that we can either take Mary's outburst at face value and impose a punitive measure upon her, likely*

> *to be something that would isolate her from the home's community, or alternatively see her behaviour as self-destructive; and the symptom of her precarious mental and emotional state. Recognising Mary's aggression to be an expression of an internal battle revealed Michelle to be a conduit for Mary's own self-loathing. She was projecting her uncontainable, uncomfortable feelings – her pain – onto a trustable person, her keyworker, a consistent source of understanding and kindness.*
>
> *Recognising that Mary was placing her worst feelings onto Michelle meant she, despite experiencing unpleasant somatic responses – a rush of adrenaline and tension in her body – could be supported to remain compassionate and to do the opposite of Mary's expectations. Michelle refused to abandon Mary, the home did not enforce a warning or other punitive action. Mary was further included and accepted as a person in need of consistent emotional support, with Michelle and her co-worker's behaviour reinforcing a connected human experience as the best way for her to feel safe.*

Understanding of psychological projection helps to protect the worker from sometimes uncomfortable experiences and to work with difficult behaviour. Mary's case shows projection as a self-defence mechanism that a person uses to protect themselves, unable to come to terms with, or fully understand or explain their destructive emotions. As we have previously noted, trauma survivors may not be able to process their emotions as successfully as others, and we must remain mindful of this when working with aggressive outbursts.

Projection can be understood through the phrase 'it's not me, it's them' – a way of placing unwanted emotions onto others. In a care home the outcome is often that 'it's the staff who are angry or at fault', 'it's the staff who are frustrated with the way I feel, not me'. Seeing the residents' actions through this lens and remaining mindful that they are trying to protect themselves from their worst emotions helps us to recognise the emotional hubris this entails. With the clarity that this knowledge brings, the PIE worker can set about embodying socially acceptable boundaries rather than being swept up in the emotional storms the resident is creating.

In Mary's case we can also use our knowledge of attachment theory and her past trauma to recognise the nastiness towards Michelle as an expression of a fear of abandonment. As the worker becomes closer to the resident there is a greater risk of loss to her and therefore a greater need to push away the caregiver.

> *'Mary, you've upset Michelle by speaking to her like that. Nobody deserves to be insulted, not you, me, or anybody.'*

> '*She can fuck off!*'
> '*Mary, I understand that accepting help can be difficult, but we need to keep everybody safe – residents and staff – nobody deserves to be insulted or shouted at.*'
> '*She's a miserable cow!*'
> '*Mary, everybody has a right to feel safe. We will continue to support you as best we can, I understand we all have good and bad days. I will say this again though, everybody deserves to feel safe.*'
> '*Alright, I'll keep it down if you piss off.*'
> *The conversation ends there. Two days later Michelle received a bunch of flowers, but no direct apology.*

In Mary's case I didn't get involved in a negative to-and-fro narrative ('she's a bitch', 'no she's not', and so on) as this would only inflame the situation, leading to a need for a 'victor', nor was she isolated (abandoned) or given a warning. I used myself as the boundary of acceptable behaviour, explaining the reasons why her language was not okay and enforcing the rules in a positive light ('we all have a right to be safe'). She was given a narrative that did not trap her in the role of aggressor ('we all have good and bad days') and it was accepted when she didn't apologise immediately (no enforced demands). That she gave Michelle flowers two days later proves the adage that actions can speak louder than words, and, most importantly, through Michelle's determination to see Mary's behaviour through a trauma-informed lens, their relationship grew stronger through this incident.

It might have been easier to enforce some sort of demand or punitive measure on Mary, but with a lifetime of painful feelings around abandonment what would we achieve? A sense of authority for the staff? What would our justification be for increasing feelings of fear in another human? That 'those are The Rules'?

The only compassionate route – the caring route – in such a situation is to reflect, respond with consideration, and to recognise the resident is in our care for a reason, primarily emotional distress.

Does elastic tolerance mean high tolerance?

So, does this mean we have to put up with bad, disruptive, or aggressive behaviour? Simply put, no. 'Elastic tolerance' does not mean 'high tolerance', it does not mean accepting aggression or anti-social behaviour as the norm, rather, it asks for thoughtful response rather than reflexive rule enforcement. 'Putting up with' infers a lack of reflection on why the behaviour is taking place, and an uncertainty around how to respond (and therefore defaulting to implementing generic rules).

'Rules are made to be broken' is a famous phrase, however Douglas MacArthur's full quote actually runs as: 'rules are mostly made to be broken and are too often for the lazy to hide behind'.[8]

This neatly sums up any situation where residents and worker refuse to work together to find a shared outcome or understanding. Where one is busy breaking the rules that the other is hiding behind, conflict is inevitable. Without a good relationship in place, rule-making is inevitably a harsh and jarring experience.

At Highwater House, which is a wet environment, residents are asked not to bring in spirits:

> *A new resident comes into the home, goes into the dining room and pulls out a bottle of vodka. He puts it on the table with a flourish and begins to drink it. This attracts other residents, who join in having a drink. A worker walks through and sees the bottle on the table.*
> *'No, you can't drink spirits in the building'*
> *'Why?'*
> *'Because it's against the rules. The rules are no spirits.'*

The resident begins to fight the 'faceless' system, attacking the obvious point of authority – the worker. Having spent years revolving between different institutions with varying types of rule enforcement it has become an almost reflexive action to push buttons. There is an impulsive striving for a sense of autonomy, and, sometimes, it's simply a habit caused by institutionalised boredom. 'Rules are there to be broken', especially if they are perceived to be overly restrictive – this reflexive rebellion is called counterwill,[9] an instinctive resistance to any sense of coercion, rife amongst adult in care services.

Then the worker, who has good knowledge of The Rules, a strong sense of professional determinism, and who believes in discipline, begins to impose restrictions in the face of the residents' counterwill. Rules are black and white, clear, and there to be enforced. If we bend the rules there might be chaos, is the logic.

The resident and the worker end up with scant respect for each other, both fulfilling their roles of rule-maker and rule-breaker. Neither role is creative nor positive; both place the people involved in a negative light.

In this scenario the worker has imposed rules without explanation of why they are doing so (which is, remember, to keep the resident safe).

The narrative of 'safety' can be understood by both worker and resident, and gives the opportunity for the worker to create a positive narrative around why they are restricting the residents' actions.

> *'Please don't drink spirits in the building'*
> *'Why?'*

'Because spirits get everyone too drunk and it becomes unsafe. People might fall and hurt themselves. We have a duty to keep everyone safe here. You are quite welcome to drink outside, or to have cider in here.'

This provides a reasonable explanation and a point of agreement.

The language we use, the route we take to achieve our goals as workers matter. They affect the way residents feel in their own home and how they bond with you.

Boundaries not rules. Inhabit not inhibit

There is a distinction between rules and boundaries. Rules restrict and control people's behaviour, and are primarily enforced with negative consequences (sanctions of some sort). Rules are external, rigid, and mechanistic (if X happens then Y happens), and can easily be experienced as punishment. For people experiencing the long-lasting effects of abuse, or who have spent time in prison or the mental health wards, punishment will likely increase fear and result in withdrawal from the carer's support.

Boundaries are guidelines or limits embodied by people. They are a set of values we aspire towards rather than a set of restrictions to avoid. As workers, we instil boundaries through our behaviour and reward positive problem solving in our clients. With boundaries we incentivise rather than sanction, and therefore make it appealing to engage.

Boundaries then are more flexible than rules. They are the 'limit of something abstract, especially a subject or sphere of activity',[10] they allow the worker greater freedom to work with anti-social behaviour by exemplifying a prosocial attitude. As we have discovered in previous chapters, the time workers spend with residents, and creating value in those relationships is the primary goal. This bond provides a reward system where time spent together *is* the reward; an achievement, catharsis, and enjoyment of human connection and greater stability.

This, then, is an important distinction, and key to working positively with our residents – our aim is to *inhabit* behaviour showing strong social boundaries using ourselves as examples, not to *inhibit* behaviour through punitive rule enforcement.

Bandura (1977) showed that good examples provided by high-status role models will be followed, but that the same is true for bad examples. Care staff have authority in the home and are therefore influential and 'high status'. How we behave *will* affect those in our care, we can use this role to inspire collectivism and strong moral values in our residents, improving their social capabilities and reducing isolation. By doing so we are modelling prosocial behaviour rather than inhibiting anti-social behaviour. This is much more beneficial than the short-term 'winning' of rule enforcement.

Creating an environment that is contained by boundaries and not defined by rules asks that the worker is intuitive in their approach, asks them to involve the residents in a shared narrative and to take risks. It may be that some staff find this approach difficult to begin with, preferring the black and white of dictatorial rules, but the positives far outweigh any concerns, which can be explored in supervision. Some outcomes we have noted at Highwater House are:

- The breaking down of professional worker/professional patient role
- Increasing trust in the resident to make positive decisions
- The environment has become based on shared values
- A great reduction in conflict and the need to police behaviour
- Residents 'self-seed' our shared values, increasing peer support

Time-outs

A key aim of elastic tolerance is to avoid eviction, and the constant passing on of 'problem' clients from service to service, or service to street. Instilling flexible boundaries rather than rigid rules supports this aim. Sometimes behaviour can become so anti-social that the client begins to put their placement at risk if they stay in the building. Examples might be threatening to throw a chair at staff, to break windows or punch another resident. If the threat is deemed to be serious (it is often only bluster caused by shame or social embarrassment – the worker should be intuitive as to how intent the resident is to do actual harm) and giving the resident a choice to calm down isn't working then other measures will need to be used. Remember, our primary aim is to keep the resident safe, and allowing their behaviour to escalate to the point of eviction does not fulfil this goal. Being evicted is the least safe, emotionally and physically, that a resident can ever be.

At Highwater House we use graded time-outs to work with this type of behaviour. Ensuring the resident is always given the choice to calm down and the chance to redress any ills is an important feature of the process.

Time-outs are exclusions from the building to give the resident a chance to calm down and reflect, it removes them from a situation where they might cause damage or harm to themselves or others. At no point should time-outs be used in a reflexive or punitive manner; they should be used as a last resort, and as part of a wider package of behavioural support. At Highwater we find that, if a resident is becoming increasingly aggressive, a cup of tea and being listened to by a trusted worker is more often than not the answer, even in very explosive situations. Using optimistic and solution-focussed language, creating a narrative of success and separating the behaviour from the person gives them the opportunity to 'win'. We recognise that feelings of tension and rage are part of the human condition and cannot be suppressed, only accepted and moderated.

Time-outs can work as controlled exposure for the resident; a brief, contained connection to their fear of abandonment coupled with a realisation that they are, despite behaving in a very challenging or disruptive way, ultimately accepted in the community. It is likely that a client's life experience will have led them to believe that after a flare up they will be punished by being emotionally isolated; and they are likely to test this reality repeatedly. Our understanding of attachment theory ensures we use time-outs to lead the resident from an expectation of abandonment (through eviction) to an expectation of inclusion (choosing to moderate behaviour). Over time the need for time-outs will reduce as they begin to believe they will be authentically cared for. In the case study of Sean, as follows, there were numerous time-outs used before he finally accepted that he was cared for.

Using the PIE approach has had great impact on our use of time-outs, as the statistics in the table show. We began to use the PIE principles in 2017, where you can see a notable reduction in time-outs, use of police, and other untoward incidents.

Event	2016	2017	2018	2019
2-hour time-out	104	68	60	48
24-hour time-out	7	2	2	2
Police called by staff	28	14	2	3
Untoward incident	67	53	20	18

It is important to promote the message that any exclusions of challenging residents are also *inclusions* for those who are not behaving anti-socially. The negative behaviour of one resident can prove the positive behaviour of another. This narrative of inclusion and success helps support residents trying their best to moderate feelings of frustration, and we can applaud their efforts as they don't react to, or follow, the disruptive resident.

The care structure as a traumatic experience

The care home is a complex environment full of guidelines, and one the resident may find difficult to negotiate. Workers may, for example, think a 'simple' ten golden rules list or the like is an accessible and clear way of communicating expectations in the home. A resident however might find this difficult, feel ashamed to say they haven't fully understood them, or, as is true for many residents at Highwater, find it hard to read or struggle with recall.

Later, if staff impose one or more of these rules – to them, using legitimate authority, after all the resident has seen them – the resident might become angry and confused, especially if they have been using substances or alcohol. If workers do not remain mindful of this possibility, residents might be 'blamed' for their behaviour, rather than supported to live within the home's boundaries.

To combat this scenario staff should regularly verbalise boundaries. This will help reduce confusion that may occur around basic expectations.

At Highwater House we have reduced the 'rules' down to two. These are:

- No violence to people or property
- No drugs on the premises

Of course, there are inevitably many more restrictions and expectations than this, however, boiled down, these are the baseline. Simple, memorable, understandable, acceptable.

Even as we remain mindful of the effects excessive rules might have on a resident, and adapt the service to reduce them or their impact, there are daily routines around the home that will also be experienced by the resident as rules and, as such, points of discipline. These incidental rules, such as medication times or meal times, should be recognised by the staff as points of potential conflict, and it should be accepted that residents may use them to prove their individual power over the system. If 'the hunger strike is the ultimate expression of resistance',[11] refusing food or medication is, whilst self-damaging, active resistance to perceived excessive authority.

> Because of their characteristic difficulties in close relationships [survivors of trauma] are particularly vulnerable to re-victimization by care givers. They may become engaged in ongoing, destructive interactions, in which the medical or mental health system replicates the behaviour of the abusive family.[12]

And so, the structure of the helping, caring environment may unintentionally retraumatise the client.

Sean was given up by his parents at around four years old. They had a very dysfunctional relationship and were abusive to each other and their children. Sean was placed in a care home with intermittent contact with his family – his older sibling had stayed with his mum when his parents broke up, a source of great pain in Sean's life. Throughout his childhood Sean's parents used him as a tool in their arguments, sometimes taking him home and treating him well, and then abruptly sending him back into care. This pattern meant he had no security, no secure base – the love was given and taken on a whim when one parent wanted to hurt the other. Inevitably this created in Sean mistrust, fear and anger that framed his teenage and adult life. At 16, as a care leaver, Sean followed a typical trajectory of drug use, petty crime and violence until he found himself, in full-blown paranoid psychosis, holding a knife up to someone's throat. His next experience of state care was prison.

This cycle continued for a number of years – a dependence on the state for money and medication, whilst experiencing the sharp edge of state care – acute mental health wards and prison.

Finally, he came to Highwater House and was sincerely welcomed with the offer of consistent human warmth. Unsurprisingly he rejected it, often violently – the fury of his lived experience, the mistrust of care settings, the yearning for parental love, all combined with the shame of needing care as a young man of 30, the fear of losing that care and the persistent paranoia caused by the self-abusive use of drugs.

Sean would regularly refuse his medication saying he would 'bang up heroin and street drugs' to 'show staff' instead, and that he would 'go over' – threatening to overdose as a source of power. He often refused meals, but would walk into the dining room at mealtimes to shout about how bad the food was, calling the staff 'gannets' for eating dinner with other residents. At times he walked into the building smoking cannabis and, when challenged, threatened the staff – he was in a continuous fight with, and held deep feelings of distress about, 'the system'. He was willing us, challenging us, to evict him and prove his unlovability.

Inevitably Sean found himself on many time-outs over the years, but he was always accepted back into the building with no strict restrictions or other punitive measures put in place. He was always greeted with respect and was always given reasons why he had to be excluded (a narrative of safety for all).

Over time he accepted the care that staff offered, and his outbursts became less frequent and less volatile. He began to, in the main, live within the boundaries embodied by the team, and recognised the need for not only the residents but the staff to feel safe. We had successfully humanised the system and separated Sean from his behaviour, thus allowing him to change into the person he should always have been – introspective, caring, and forthright.

We could tell the boundaries were accepted when he began to place them upon himself. Once, during an impulsive, volatile outburst he *shouted, 'Yeah, yeah, I'll go out, just watch me!' and he did, until he had calmed down. This was a significant shift towards self-soothing and accepting reasonable boundaries in the home, and was the start of him no longer needing time-outs.*

It took a long time to build a trusting relationship with Sean, his default to violence proved to be a struggle for even the most skilled in the team, however, the violent, aggressive outbursts could not be seen in any other context than that of a deeply troubled, struggling child.

In Sean's case the care home was a symbol of shame, of containment (like a prison), of the system he began hating as a child (taking him away from his parents), the proffered care seen as dangerous and threatening, in his traumatised state of hypervigilant mistrust.

Our care – meant with sincerity, given with compassion – was retraumatising Sean. An upsetting situation for both the resident and staff. If a resident has been through the care system as a child, the PIE worker should be especially aware that there may be a reaction within the adult returning to a care environment. An environment which, with its routines and power, imbalance will have caused or added to that individual's trauma, and respond to the ensuing behaviour – the anger and rage – with compassion, consistent boundaries, and understanding.

In Sean's case the Cognitive Behavioural Therapy (CBT) model helped staff in their work – it was a useful psychological lens for them to further their ability to care for an often-volatile man. The CBT model, developed by Aaron Beck in the 1960s, has become one of the most well-known therapeutic tools in use today. It is famously depicted as a triangle, with each point representing a key area of the human experience: behaviour, thoughts, and feelings. Each of the three affects the other areas. In working with difficult behaviour, it is also useful to envisage only the tip of the triangle being visible with the rest of the triangle buried out of sight. The tip of the triangle represents behaviour. The other two hidden areas are the internal aspects of the model – thoughts and feelings – and they can only be seen or accessed via the external behaviour.

If workers respond to or try to work with only the visible behaviour without taking into account the driving forces of emotion or thought, their actions will inevitably become increasingly punitive in response to Sean's aggression. As Sean's internal needs are left unanswered, his behaviour, an attempt to communicate this internal unrest and driven by uncomfortable feelings, becomes more erratic, and so more enforcement is needed. This cycle is destructive for both Sean and the workers and does not allow a relationship to develop. As the distance between Sean and the carers increases, they become seen only as 'enforcers' and he fulfills the role of 'disruptive resident' until the placement breaks down – often dramatically and possibly leading to the ultimate punitive measure – prison time – for the resident. Unless the drivers to the behaviour are worked with, Sean's sense of isolation will only increase, the experience of living in care once again becoming a source of pain, the very opposite of its intention.

Whilst it is not the care worker's role to provide counselling, it is their lot to provide security and a trustable environment, that is, to answer the resident's internal needs and to help them find balance.

So, in answer to aggression and volatile behaviour from Sean we should accept that he is projecting, much like Mary whom we met earlier, his unpleasant feelings onto the worker and the home, feelings which are valid and should be accepted. In the face of his explosive temper we can embody fair boundaries, repeated calmly, remembering his greatest fears are abandonment and lack of security. We can also accept our own somatic responses as authentic; after all, being yelled at is not pleasant and will invoke a reaction.

Sean's case, as with Stu's, highlights that there is a difference between 'difficult' and 'dangerous' behaviour. The Care Act's principle of proportionality can be reflected upon here. The staff team must be ready, sometimes despite their own somatic response, to delineate between these stages of behaviour and to only enact sanctions, rules, or reinforcements suitable to that particular occasion. For Sean this meant a choice to go to his room to calm down if he was shouting, a time-out if he was becoming more threatening, or a longer time-out if he was really aggressive and needed more time to become calm and reflect. This graded approach helped him to recognise nuance in his own behaviour, and for him to not feel persecuted. Blanket bans or evictions from a service, with little intuitive process informing them, creates black and white thinking in both the staff and client, and polarises behaviour – with both playing the victim and perpetrator roles.

We should question whether a situation is 'difficult' or 'dangerous' when working with anti-social behaviour, and whilst a difficult situation may become dangerous and vice versa, the more that workers trust themselves, the more confident, and capable, they will become. Having witnessed many hundreds of interactions involving conflict, it is clear that the behaviour involved is more often than not difficult, demanding, defiant, or disruptive, but not dangerous.

As we have previously explored, a resident's risk assessment might create bias in the worker and unfairly inform their response to a moment of aggression; the worker should remain mindful of this and aim to guard against it. A calm and considered – that is, reflective – response will lead to an outcome where both parties have 'succeeded' by promoting joint ownership over the environment and a shared, acceptable outcome.

Peer support

Peer support and group dynamics play an important role in moderating individuals' behaviour. A sense of belonging and self-agency is recognised as key in the process of recovery from trauma; therefore, where possible, workers should facilitate spaces for a group dynamic to grow and self-manage. Healing, and therefore reduction of anti-social behaviour, best takes place in a communal setting. Behavioural management, imposed by an authority figure, inevitably brings into question the resident's autonomy; if psychological trauma is an 'affliction of the powerless',[13] returning power to the individual and group is paramount to support growth. Staff should broker relationships between residents whose mutual support will be invaluable.

Bourne writes that in incidents involving groups of people you have a pre-existing relationship with, much of the work will be done before the incident takes place: 'if each service user can sense you are competent, can demonstrate absolutely clear . . . boundaries and have a genuine interest in them as a person then you will be in a good position to deal with anything that arises'.[14] He goes on to introduce 'patterning' – a way in which a staff member can help a group dynamic using non-verbal cues to direct it towards a positive outcome. This again relies on confidence, trust, and rapport built through strong relationships with the clients, but, most of all, this can only happen whilst sharing a physical space with the residents.

As we have already seen, Banduras' social learning theory shows people are affected by and will follow behaviour of others in their environment; they also effect the environment themselves. As PIE workers who spend as much time as possible in a shared environment with clients, forging strong bonds, this means the importance of the way we act amongst the home's peer group cannot be exaggerated.

As we take part in the communal environment, we share emotional contagion: 'The tendency to automatically mimic and synchronize facial expressions, vocalizations, postures, and movements with those of another person's and, consequently, to converge emotionally.'[15]

As workers mindfully embody positive behavioural boundaries and promote a calm, reflective environment, so too will the residents. Over time, this development of a calm environment will self-seed via the resident peer group. I have noted that often there is, as in Stu's case above, a sense of relief when a resident no longer needs to upkeep a faux aggression or provocative stance. This relaxing affects the 'feel' of the whole building. We know that a common symptom of trauma is hypervigilance, and also a symptom of many mental health issues (such as anxiety). As new residents join the home they will sense and reflect the atmosphere, especially when it is being willingly embodied rather than enforced.

The peer group, with support, will manage itself, and the worker can change their role from rule-maker to mediator. The worker must however trust the group to self-soothe – to communally instil the collective boundaries – without overt intervention of an 'authoritarian' worker. The aim of communal living is not total calm, constantly – that would be an artificially high, unattainable expectation upon a group of people living together – but it is for a client to willingly moderate their behaviour in order to take some part in the peer group.

Our primary objectives of keeping residents safe and avoiding retraumatisation are best answered through peer support and communal living. Remembering that behaviour is communication, 'a vocabulary of experience',[16] and that people cannot heal in isolation, workers must learn to recognise and speak the verbal and physical cues and language of trauma. With shared vision, consistency, and understanding, that language will become spoken.

The north wind and the sun

Elastic tolerance can, in many ways, be summed up by the moral story of the north wind and the sun:

> *There was once an argument between the north wind and the sun about who was stronger. They argued for some time but neither of them emerged the winner.*
>
> *It was then they spotted a man walking down the road wearing a coat. They challenged each other to make the man remove his coat – the winner would be declared the strongest.*
>
> *The north wind went first, blowing a stronger and stronger gale, using all his might to force the coat from the man. Yet the man just clutched his coat more firmly around him, until finally the wind became exhausted, his efforts futile.*
>
> *Next the sun took his turn. He gently shone down on the man, expending little energy. The man, surprised at the weather change soon began to warm up. Within a short while he chose to remove his coat.*
>
> *The sun was declared the strongest, and the winner.*

Persuasion works better than force, and helping residents to make positive choices about their behaviour is, in the end, the most effective way of managing challenging behaviour.

> This chapter has reflected KLOES:
>
> S1
>
> - 'People are involved in developing a comprehensive and innovative approach to safeguarding, which enables positive risk-taking to maximise their control over their lives.'
>
> S2
>
> - 'There is a transparent and open culture that encourages creative thinking in relation to people's safety.'
> - 'People are enabled to take positive risks to maximise their control over their care and support.'
> - 'Staff show empathy and have an enabling attitude that encourages people to challenge themselves, while recognising and respecting their lifestyle choices.'
> - 'The service helps people have a meaningful life by using imaginative or innovative ways to manage risk, while supporting people to stay safe.'
>
> S3
>
> - 'Staff proactively anticipate and mitigate risks to people's safety and feel their skills are being used effectively.'
>
> E7
>
> - 'The service has a very flexible approach to any restrictions it imposes on people; keeping them under constant review, making them in a time-limited way, and only when absolutely necessary.'

Notes

1 www.lexico.com/en
2 www.therapeuticcommunities.org/wp-content/uploads/2014/07/whiteley.pdf
3 www.ncbi.nlm.nih.gov/pmc/articles/PMC2791894/
4 Bourne, I., *Facing Danger in the Helping Professions* (Open University Press, 2013), 57.
5 Section 1.3.13–1.3.17 www.nice.org.uk/guidance/ng10/chapter/1-Recommendations#preventing-violence-and-aggression-2

74 *Elastic tolerance*

6 www.narrativeapproaches.com/resources/quotes/
7 https://s3.amazonaws.com/academia.edu.documents/42932840/Homelessness_as_psychological_trauma._Br20160222-27441-5zayw9.pdf?response-content-disposition=inline%3B%20filename%3DHomelessness_as_psychological_trauma_Bro.pdf&X-Amz-Algorithm=AWS4-HMAC-SHA256&X-Amz-Credential=AKIAIWOWYYGZ2Y53UL3A%2F20190904%2Fus-east-1%2Fs3%2Faws4_request&X-Amz-Date=20190904T093606Z&X-Amz-Expires=3600&X-Amz-SignedHeaders=host&X-Amz-Signature=d03809ce58bc538b9a2d15345542ffe3be30ce2e8b2f76b56ec5fa240b39a1c4
8 www.bartleby.com/73/1649.html
9 https://en.wikipedia.org/wiki/Counterwill
10 www.lexico.com/en/definition/boundary
11 Herman, J., *Trauma and Recovery* (Basic Books, 1997), 79.
12 Herman, *Trauma and Recovery*, 123.
13 Herman, *Trauma and Recovery*, 33.
14 Bourne, *Facing Danger in the Helping Professions*, 178.
15 www.neurohumanitiestudies.eu/archivio/Emotional_Contagion.pdf
16 Cockersell, P. (Ed.), *Social Exclusion, Compound Trauma and Recovery* (Jessica Kingsley Books, 2018), 31.

7 Psychological awareness

> In this chapter we will:
>
> - Find improving psychological awareness supports the worker to remain resilient
> - See that workers are not 'pseudo-psychiatrists', but use their knowledge to improve care
> - Explore how trauma can affect residents' behaviour
> - Explore how using the system and being given multiple diagnoses can be a disempowering process

Introduction

Over the coming chapters we are introduced to the five key elements of a PIE and explore how they can be used in the registered care home.

To re-cap, our Psychologically Informed Environment – Residential model is:

- Psychological awareness
- Environment
- Evidence
- Rules, roles, and responsiveness
- Staff support and training

Kindness: 'the quality of being friendly, generous, and considerate'

Kindness, empathy, and perseverance are the carers' primary tools. Residents in our care come to rely upon us as consistent figures in their lives, fulfilling the role of friend, advocate, and supporter. Carers, then, have a duty to provide for and shape this dynamic process, ensuring they routinely promote a message of support and compassion. To do so they must be able to sustain a steady flow of positive support, even in difficult or upsetting moments. To guard against compassion fatigue, carers must build resilience; when providing care for those with a mental illness or substance misuse issues, that resilience is born from knowledge.

It must be stressed that in a PIE our aim is not to become 'pseudo-psychiatrists', rather, it is to enhance our ability to remain kind and empathic in the face of emotional upheaval, challenging behaviour, and human suffering and for us to improve our skills as carers so we can provide truly authentic connections without fear or experiencing undue personal harm.

Rogers writes:

> Can I let myself experience positive attitudes towards this other person – attitudes of warmth, caring, liking, interest, respect? It is not easy . . . We are afraid that if we let ourselves freely experience these positive feelings towards another, we may be trapped by them. They may lead to demands on us or we may be disappointed in our trust, and these outcomes we fear. So, as a reaction we tend to build up distance between ourselves and others – aloofness, a 'professional' attitude, an impersonal relationship.[1]

Improving psychological awareness helps carers to better understand the complex behaviour of their clients and to understand its drivers. This in turn allows the workers to create authentic, trusting bonds. There is no doubt that working with revolving door clients, entrenched in the psychiatric system, can be tiring, and that connecting with erratic substance users can be disheartening. However, improved understanding of why people choose to take their drug of choice, of why a resident might be refusing a good meal, or why they are behaving in such a self-defeating manner helps to create in carers (and the service) a narrative of acceptance and hope.

> *Harry is spinning around in the foyer like a spinning top, dragging his bare feet and picking and scratching at his arm. His skin is a greenish-grey and he has deep black rings under his eyes; his hands and feet are dirty. He has just been vomiting on the street outside the home and his clothes are stained. He isn't making a lot of sense – just saying garbled words. He has just got back from a house somewhere in the city where he has injected heroin, his drug of choice.*
>
> *Over the course of the night Harry will vomit and bring up bile all over his bedroom floor, he'll drop ash, cigarettes and rubbish, and when he's spinning around in his room throw coffee up the walls.*

This is a regular pattern of behaviour, and for the domestic and care team it is a constant job to keep Harry and his room clean.

Harry's behaviour is erratic, dangerous, and frustrating. The ongoing battle to keep the environment clean and to support Harry can inevitably be wearing.

To successfully remain caring, and to avoid burnout, we need to frame Harry's behaviour as purposeful, if self-defeating.

Harry is diagnosed with paranoid schizophrenia and Asperger's (he would now be diagnosed as on the autism spectrum disorder in the DSM-V). After the sudden onset of psychosis, he spent much of his late teens and early twenties in and out of mental health wards as various professionals attempted to stabilise his symptoms. At some point Harry discovered that heroin made him feel less anxious and subdued the worst of his symptoms. As a man with Asperger's who found difficulty interacting socially, heroin helped answer many of his needs. For Harry the sudden and acute symptoms of psychosis, and the placement on a ward under section, was also a traumatic incident – fracturing and destabilising – again heroin helped soothe the stress caused by this event.

When talking about Harry's lack of self-care one day, Carol, one of our domestic team, asked why anybody would do that to themselves? Why would anyone choose to get themselves into Harry's state?

It is helpful for Carol to have Harry's behaviour framed through the Self-Medication Hypothesis – that Harry's heroin use is his best attempt to control his positive schizophrenic symptoms and the agitation he feels. Opiates 'can have dramatic and dampening effect on angry and rageful feelings. They can make a person who feels unhinged by irritable and agitated feelings suddenly feel calm and mellow.'[2] It is easy then to see why Harry uses heroin.

Harry's life experience can also be seen through a trauma-informed lens. If trauma is 'an event, series of events, or set of circumstances that is experienced by an individual as physically or emotionally harmful or life threatening and that has lasting adverse effects on the individuals functioning and mental, physical, social, emotional or spiritual wellbeing',[3] then Harry's experiences are traumatic. Having the knowledge that responses to trauma can involve feelings of hyperarousal, anxiety, and self-destructive behaviour, we can see why Harry might use heroin to regulate himself.

Recognising Harry's drug taking is not simply a biological addiction (although that plays a part) which he 'just needs to stop', and that his behaviour is complex and informed by his traumatic experience, is an important step towards staff remaining resilient, and able to provide authentic care.

It reduces the chances that staff might 'blame' Harry for his challenging behaviour, a necessity when supporting such a vulnerable client.

Highwater House

In 2016 we chose a psychological framework of Trauma-Informed Care and Dialectal Behavioural Therapy (DBT) to use at Highwater House. Having worked with substance misuse for many years most of the team had previously attended training on cognitive behavioural therapy, motivational interviewing, and the cycle of change. Indeed, we are fortunate to have a long-serving staff team at Highwater – most of whom have been in service for 15 years or more. The variety of skills and experiences that this brings to the table is vast, and its worth cannot be overstated.

We bought in training on both of our chosen frameworks which were received well by staff, and yet it quickly became clear that the idea of using a unifying model (DBT) wasn't going to work. Whether it was the varied type of resident we support or the staff having a wide range of prior knowledge we'll never know, but the approach which suited Highwater House was much less neat, more piecemeal.

Our journey at Highwater then reflected the changes being made at that time between the classic model of PIE and PIE 2.0 – the move from having a psychological 'framework' to having psychological 'awareness'. Feedback from other services across the UK around the realities of putting theory into practice were possibly informing this change.

We wanted our frontline to be able to pull from a variety of theories to help them fulfil their duties as carers. For us, the psychological theory had to underpin simple compassion, and support kindness rather than place any pressure on staff to abide by a set of theoretical principles.

The training on Trauma-Informed Care resonated much more deeply within the team – and trauma-informed practice has permeated our care provision at Highwater House. However, our daily practice as carers at Highwater House draws as much from CBT and the Self-Medication Hypothesis as Trauma-Informed Care.

And so, using one specific psychological framework has not gained traction at Highwater House, rather, we have been putting together a jigsaw puzzle of many useful psychological tools to suit our residents and staff. I consider us to be a magpie service. Our journey has been, and continues to be, an exploration of light-bulb moments and dead ends, of knowing when one narrative 'fits' and another doesn't. Every PIE will inevitably use whatever tools they need to support their client group; a slightly messy process, but certainly reflective of the complexity of caring for fellow humans.

Indeed, if I was to be asked to pin down a framework, I would choose to answer in emotional terms; and give examples of our work using emotional language. I would suggest workers use a framework of kindness, empathy and emotional literacy which is *supported* by trauma-informed practice and psychological theory.

This approach also suits the care environment's many workers. From domestics to managers, everybody can speak in terms of kindness and compassion. It might not be suitable for all workers to receive training on psychological theory. I believe, though, that there is a tipping point where enough team members are recognising, using and verbalising trauma-informed practice for it to encase the whole service. This then works as a herd immunisation against vicarious trauma, burnout, and compassion fatigue; and becomes self-seeding.

The magpie approach

Below is a non-exhaustive list of key theories and approaches we have found useful at Highwater House:

- Trauma-Informed Care
- The Self-Medication Hypothesis
- Attachment Theory
- Narrative Therapy
- Pre-Treatment Pathways
- CBT
- Motivational Interview Techniques
- The Cycle of Change
- Pro-Social Modelling
- Emotional Literacy
- Operant Conditioning
- Reciprocal Determinism
- Mentalization

Care homes, PIEs, and fractured identities

There is a clear distinction between the 'usual' clients of a PIE – the framework has been primarily used amongst the homeless community – and working age adults in residential care; that is, residents in care will necessarily have been through a risk and needs assessment and had contact with social and psychiatric services whereas a homeless client may not.

The certainty that our residents have been part of the human services system means our focus should often be upon extricating them from routine professional patient-ism, and using our psychological awareness to heal the fracturing that can occur in individuals as they negotiate their way through multiple helping services and all of their idiosyncratic assessments. Earlier, in Chapter 2, we met Rob as he attended a Section 117 meeting with five professionals, all with different goals and bias. Each service needed Rob to behave and relate in a specified way – with the onus on his ability to fit the system rather than the other way around. He had therefore collected multiple diagnoses throughout his life. Thus, probation needed him to repent his criminality; substance misuse services needed him to prove a trajectory towards sobriety; mental health services needed him to prove insight into his condition and remain behaviourally stable; and so on. The current focus on single-use services with the clients being part of a purchaser/provider relationship defies the reality that people with complex needs will often find it difficult to negotiate the multi-faceted system. In Rob's case he wasn't sure what day of the week it was, let alone whether he should be attending, and pleased to be the focus of, a multi-disciplinary meeting.

High levels of contact with multiple parts of the system can be an abrasive experience, with this friction causing feelings of paranoia, anger, and powerlessness. Our clients, particularly those with tri-morbidity, are buffeted around the system and asked to repeatedly use different parts of their life experience (often stories of abuse and neglect) as currency to purchase care, or procure medication and benefits. In a PIE care home, a key function is to give people the room to step back from their multiple diagnoses and re-frame themselves as a whole human being; it is a protective space. We are not a clinic or ward, a treatment centre or surgery – we are a home, plain and simple, where people can be 'themselves' and experiment with being more than a collection of their assessments. Rogers writes: 'If I accept the person as something fixed, already diagnosed and classified, already shaped by his past, then I am doing my part to confirm this limited hypothesis. If I accept him as a process of becoming then I am doing what I can to confirm or make real his potentialities.'[4] In a care home we can use our psychological awareness to give the resident time to embark upon this process, supporting them to explore the space between and beyond their diagnoses – the mundane, the comical, the assertive sides to themselves, without being constantly assessed.

It is the care home's non-clinical environment and non-clinical workers that can promote a more human story. Narrative therapy determines that the dominant story is not the whole story – humans are 'multi-storied', and stories change over time. Professional bias (the role of 'complete' psychiatrist will expect a client to become a 'complete' patient, for example), and strict entry criteria to services can bind individuals to a narrative thread that restricts their personal growth, or movement towards homeostasis.

In her essay on trauma-informed practice in services, 'The Opposite of Violence', Carlyn Zwarenstein explores her personal experience of mental illness, and her hope for kindness in the support offered:

> An image that comes to me again and again is that of the survivor of a fire or a car accident who we see so often in the movies, sitting near the scene of the incident, wrapped in a thermal or fuzzy blanket, head bent gratefully over a mug of hot tea or cocoa while someone – anyone – speaks to them kindly. Not better, but safe, comforted, in a holding situation from which healing can arise. For me, mental distress most often takes the form of depression, or hopelessness, or extreme low mood, and when I have felt at my worst, it is to that comforting image that I cling.[5]

She goes on to say that 'kindness is an expression of empathy in settings invariably freighted with power imbalances' – as a care home is.

Redressing the power imbalance between worker and resident is a crucial challenge for care home staff. Recognising the imbalance exists at all is our first step. We separate ourselves into roles – the carer and cared for, the well and the ill, the helpful and helpless – that speaks volumes about where power lies.

Gabor Maté notes, about his substance using patients:

> much as I want to accept them, some days I find myself full of disapproval and judgement . . . it is my problem except that given the power imbalance between us, it's all too easy to make it their problem.[6]

Working on frontline human services, and recognising that interacting with the system can be a traumatising and dislocating process, staff *need* the knowledge that trauma survivors are 'particularly vulnerable to revictimization by care-givers. They may become engaged in on-going destructive interactions, in which the medical or mental health system replicates the behaviour of the abusive family';[7] they *need* to recognise that 'individuals susceptible to addiction do not adequately recognise, tolerate or express their feelings, because they struggle with problems in self-esteem, relationships and self-care';[8] they *need* the skills to distinguish between dangerous behaviour and that of traumatised and lost individuals.

Equally, they should, through their psychological awareness, know that 'recovery can only take place in the context of relationships';[9] that 'secure attachment relationships provide our best means of ameliorating emotional distress';[10] and that with time and support people can move beyond their diagnosis and live a more comprehensive human experience.

This chapter has reflected KLOES:

S1

- 'The service is particularly creative in the way it involves and works with people to understand their diverse circumstances and individual needs. It challenges discrimination and encourages staff, people who use the service and others to do the same.'

S2

- 'Staff show empathy and have an enabling attitude that encourages people to challenge themselves, while recognising and respecting their lifestyle choices.'

E1

- 'The service . . . keeps up to date with new research and development to make sure staff are trained to follow best practice.'
- 'Staff training is developed and delivered around individual needs.'

C1

- 'There is a strong, visible person-centred culture.'

R1

- 'The service understands the needs of different people and groups of people, and delivers care in a way that that meets these needs.'

W1

- 'The service's vision and values are imaginative and are at the heart of the service.'

Notes

1. Rogers, C. R., *On Becoming a Person* (Constable, 2004), 52.
2. Khanzian, E. J. and Albanese, M. J., *Understanding Addiction as Self-Medication* (Good Time Books, 2013), 66.
3. Sourced from https://store.samhsa.gov/system/files/sma14-4884.pdf, 7.
4. Rogers, *On Becoming a Person*, 55.
5. Daley, A., Costa, L. and Beresford, P. (Eds.), *Madness, Violence, and Power* (University of Toronto Press, 2019), 50.

6 Maté, G., *In the Realm of the Hungry Ghosts* (Vermillion, 2018), 13.
7 Herman, J., *Trauma and Recovery* (Basic Books, 1997), 123.
8 Khanzian and Albanese, *Understanding Addiction*, 37.
9 Herman, *Trauma and Recovery*, 133.
10 Cockersell, P. (Ed.), *Social Exclusion, Compound Trauma and Recovery* (Jessica Kingsley Publishers 2018), 115.

8 Environment

> In this chapter we will:
>
> - Discover the environment can be a tool for change
> - See how workers' use of the environment affects residents
> - Discover sharing spaces empowers residents
> - Explore changes to a service which are 'low cost, high impact'
> - See mealtimes as a key area to make positive change

Environment – 'the complex of physical, chemical, and biotic factors (such as climate, soil, and living things) that act upon an organism or an ecological community and ultimately determine its form and survival'.[1]

We do not think of the residential care home as a threatening environment. The care home's purpose, to provide benign and supportive care, places it as the antithesis of an intimidating or hostile setting. Yet, despite workers' best intentions, the care environment can reinforce, compound or create trauma in residents. SAMSHA's 2014 *Guidance for a Trauma-Informed Approach* states: 'Staff who work within a trauma-informed environment are taught to recognize how organizational practices may trigger painful memories and retraumatize clients with trauma histories.'[2] The very act of caring, if provided in a mechanistic or institutionalised manner, may trigger past trauma. The aim in a PIE is, at the very least, to actively resist retraumatisation as workers provide their care. Maté writes about working with addicts, 'If we are to help . . . we must strive to change not them, but their environments. These are the only things we *can* change.'[3]

Care homes must comply with a strict set of regulations and work within a complex framework of legislation. This necessary compliance can lead to an incidental bias within the home, where fulfilling the daily duties and tasks take precedence over less regulated, or less easily monitored, aspects of care giving, such as creating quality connection with residents. The Care Act's focus on a person-centred, strengths-based approach to providing care raises the prospect of parity between emotional and physical health, yet falls short of legislating for this. Working as a PIE, placing the residents' 'thinking, emotions, personalities and past experience'[4] at the heart of the day's work, helps to redress structural bias by creating a strong person-centred narrative within the home. Indeed, Johnson and Haigh write that a definitive marker for a PIE is that staff, when asked why the unit is run in a certain way, would give an answer couched in terms of the emotional and psychological needs of the service user, rather than giving a more logistical or practical rationale such as convenience, costs, or Health and Safety regulations.[5]

How workers use their environment, then, is as important as the environment itself; their actions and intentions influence the *feel* of the home. Their use of the space can inhibit residents' personal growth and reinforce institutionalised behaviour, or help soften the edges of the system, reducing any sense of 'us and them'.

Many working age adults in care will have spent time in coercive or correctional places. At Highwater House every one of our residents has had some experience of being arrested and imprisoned, of being sectioned by the police whilst acutely mentally unwell, or spent time on secure mental health wards. There is a certainty that their contact with the system will have created an emotional response within them – too often this will be negative. Common amongst residents arriving at Highwater House is a sense of resignation that they are, despite being supported by services, not truly *included* in the service. They are using the service but not part of the service; the service belongs to the workers sitting in the office.

Spending time in locked institutions or years within the system undoubtably creates apathy; the routines and restrictions of a life defined through mental illhealth and addiction enforce a subdued passivity. It is this powerlessness that workers must be aware of as they move through their day, ensuring they do not unintentionally compound it. Services which don't proactively try to break down these patterns of institutionalisation, and give power to the individual, inadvertently take part in structural violence. Defined through social structures which perpetuate an imbalance in the system that does not allow an individual to reach their full potential: 'Structural violence is silent, it does not show – it is essentially static, it is the tranquil waters. In a static society, personal violence will be registered, whereas structural violence may be seen as about as natural as the air around us.'[6] We can easily see the angry or threatening resident – less obvious is the silent coercion that has driven this behaviour.

To guard against these almost invisible but corrosive restrictions workers must remain mindful of the residents' past experiences and use the environment to create a 'whole home' ecology defined through shared experience, shared space, and equality between workers and residents. They must strive to create balance, and support residents' self-actualisation.

Sharing space

The key aim in a PIE – to build trusting relationships – happens best if we share communal spaces with residents. For workers to create these bonds they must be prepared, and supported by managers, to break down traditional roles and to search for new ways to connect with the clients. As we have explored in previous chapters, workers with an overly 'professional' attitude can harm the residents' wellbeing – the power imbalance being inherently shaming for the client. If the only quality contact time workers have with residents is in an 'official' capacity – for example, in link-working sessions or in amongst the professional bustle of bed making, laundry duties, or cleaning – the imbalance in the relationship will remain starkly clear. It is only when the worker takes off their professional 'hat' that the best work of human connection, the root of healing, can begin. Sharing communal space is the first and easiest change to make within the home; our experience at Highwater House suggests it is this that has had the most impact. It is key to note that workers are paid for every hour they are in the home, not for every task they complete, so this intervention need not cost anything more than time. It solely relies on managers creating a narrative within the home that connecting emotionally and authentically with the clients is of equal importance as completion of physical tasks, and ensuring time is freed up for workers to do so. Therefore, the role of management in a PIE is

> to facilitate the staff to have the time to do their primary work – which, in most social care organisations is something like supporting the client in their change and recovery process – and to enable the secondary work, the administrative and service maintenance burden, to be done as efficiently as possible and with the minimum necessary interference in the performance of the primary task.[7]

At Highwater House we enabled staff to increase impromptu and informal time with the residents by creating a shared lounge where workers, without fail, spend the evenings, and other times throughout the day whenever possible. The main office is closed off to increase the sense of equality, and to ensure staff are accessible without the need for residents to knock on a door to reach them. Reducing the physical barriers, the locked doors, between workers and residents has created a greater feeling of warmth and comradeship which is palpable around the home. The shared lounge is a space where workers can embody boundaries (as discussed in the chapter on elastic tolerance) which has led to fewer rules being enforced. An outcome of this approach has been that the building feels less like a service and more like a home, meaning anxious and fearful residents, used to institutional settings, are more able to relax and accept the offered care.

It must be noted that some workers found leaving the office and spending time in the shared lounge more of a challenge, whilst others embraced the process more readily. Staff as well as residents are susceptible to institutionalisation and so some found the idea of change a struggle, and to this day still find spending impromptu, 'disorganised' time with the residents challenging. It falls on the shoulders of managers and supervisors to explain the reasons and purpose behind the change in approach, and to instil a narrative that each and every conversation is an opportunity to create incremental change in the residents' wellbeing. There is a tipping point which will be reached, where the service and team will begin to define their good work through these actions and not solely through larger 'headline' activities.

Creating a Psychologically Informed Environment created by No-one Left Out Solutions Ltd says that the objectives of a Psychologically Informed Environment are:

- 'A non-institutional, safe and welcoming service that facilitates interaction between staff and clients
- Clients have choice and control over how and when they engage
- There is a sense of physical and emotional safety for both clients and staff
- There is a culture of health and wellbeing.'[8]

Having a shared communal space has meant we have reduced the number of 'fixed' activities which many of our residents, due to paranoia and counterwill, would avoid, and replaced them with a much more organic process (the home does however still provide more formal activities as well). Staff are encouraged to bring in their own interests and hobbies to use in the lounge as prompts for conversation, and there is no pressure for residents to complete or take part in any activity. This more freewheeling approach has undoubtably created a more relaxed atmosphere, one where even the most reclusive of residents have joined us from time to time.

It is through creating a shared space, and promoting building strong connection with residents using the PIE approach as our key aim, that our yearly statistics show the number of 'meaningful interactions' between workers and residents have increased exponentially. The shared sense of ownership over the space, and freedom to come and go has meant we have engaged residents previously deemed unreachable. Our statistics show our 'pre-PIE' engagement with residents in 2016 as 918 – by 2018, two years into using the PIE principles, the figure was 3059, an almost 250% increase in meaningful contact time across two years. At the same time our use of time-outs dropped by around 50% and the number of 'untoward incidents' fell by around two-thirds. These staggering statistics prove how simple adaptions to the daily routine of carers can have wide implications on the wellbeing of the service user.

The physical building

A consistent theme throughout this book is that of power imbalance, and how workers can reduce the impact of this damaging dynamic upon residents. It is in the physical environment of the home that the workers', managers', and residents' differing needs will clash.

Torrington writes that, when designing care homes, 'commonly, the needs of the management predominate over the needs of the users, with the result that the primary users have little sense of ownership of their own territory'.[9] Furthermore, we also know that to successfully recover from trauma, to feel secure and comfortable, a person needs to feel some sense of control – initially over their physical surroundings: 'No-one can establish a safe environment alone, the task of developing an adequate safety plan always includes . . . social support.'[10]

The PIE approach asks us to look at the home environment through our residents' eyes, and to, firstly, question whose needs are being answered by it, and second, if workers can adapt the environment to better suit the clients' needs.

Creating a Psychologically Informed Environment asks that 'thoughtful consideration is given to how information is communicated; the number and placement of signs and notice boards, how messages are worded' and that 'clients and staff are consulted about the décor, lighting, use of colour'.

Using this advice at Highwater House we realised that, despite the KLOE – Safe suggesting that 'people are provided with a range of accessible information about how to keep themselves safe and how to report any issues of concern',[11] the amount of posters and information around the building could be compounding residents' prior trauma and creating an institutionalised feel to the home. Many of the signs on our noticeboards were about being vulnerable, abused, or addicted – topics that related to our client group. We had always considered that prominently displaying information about how to access other services was good practice, however, using the PIE principles we came to see that a survivor of childhood abuse, as many of our residents are, would not feel comfortable or 'at home' walking past a poster with 'Have You Been Abused?' in large writing countless times a day. They had come to the home *because* of their past experiences of abuse and the poster was doing the opposite of what it is designed for – it was creating a feeling of mistrust and anxiety. And, more corrosively, the residents did not have the power to take the poster down. This, then, is an example of the environment answering the management's, and CQC's, needs and not the residents. The solution to providing access to information around safeguarding without it being intrusive was for staff to verbalise it, to speak openly about the topic, and to build relationships where residents would feel free to speak openly if they had any concerns. This process has been documented in the home as a policy decision, and explicable in inspections through staff interviews. On safeguarding, Regulation 13 of the Health and Social Care Act (2008) Regulations (2014) (4) (d) states that 'care or treatment for service users must not be provided for in a way that is degrading for the service user or significantly disregards the needs of the service user for care or treatment'. If a resident has no agency over removing a retraumatising or triggering item within the home, this 'disregards the needs of the service user'.

At Highwater House we now have as few signs up as possible, recognising the ways in which they could reflect the power structure within the home. Signs we do use are phrased in a way to help the residents have choice and succeed in their actions. Therefore, for example, the number of no-smoking signs have been reduced (workers can verbalise the rule), and any we do have are framed in a positive way – 'please smoke in your room', rather than the more directive 'no-smoking'. It is good practice for workers to imagine walking around their own homes and to ask themselves how they would feel if there were instructions, signs, and restrictions pinned up all around it.

When exploring creating space for stress reduction:

> one key area – found in almost all buildings – is corridors. These are typically places of noise, action; and corridor noise increases agitation. Corridors also embody un-spoken power relations; doors can exclude and bar, as well as providing entrance. They are used to negotiate physically the person's progression in and through some process, their membership.[12]

I had a conversation with a resident, Andy, once. He explained a situation to me involving the resident in the room next door, George.

Andy and I are sitting in the main office having a chat when the emergency alarm goes. Andy says:
  'George waits for me to come into the office and then does that. He does it on purpose.'

> *'Does what?'*
> *He hears my door shut and then counts how long it takes for me to get into the office, then he presses his buzzer to make me leave.'*
> *'Are you sure? Why would he do that?'*
> *'Because he's jealous of me being in here.'*

Doors hold power, and the office was creating an us-and-them power struggle, between staff and residents, and between residents themselves. Andy's story, whilst patently not true, felt true to him – the emotion he was feeling was valid.

Let's meet Dan in a regular situation before we created the shared lounge –

> *Dan can be troublesome at times. He often knocks on the office door asking for medication at the wrong time. He infuriates staff with this behaviour.*
>
> *When he knocks on the door, they shout out to him, 'Dan, you know it's not meds time! You only had them an hour ago!' They know he'll knock again 'trying to get his meds early' a number of times this shift. When he's told 'no' he can become angry, shouting at the staff. He'll come to the door and peer through the glass panel before curling his lip and storming off.*
> *'Dan is capable of knowing when his next lot of meds are due'*
> *'Dan is playing us up'*
> *'He knows he can't get them early'*
> *Dan doesn't really want his medication, he is trying to find a legitimate way of accessing the office to have human contact, something he craves despite deep feelings of persecution and paranoia. On the other side of the door he feels abandoned and hates to hear laughter or conversation emanating from the office. When other residents leave the office, he swears at them and calls them 'teacher's pet' and 'suck-ups'. This often leads to conflict and a bad feeling within the home.*

For the residents in the office there was a sense of inclusion, for Dan the experience was of exclusion. With the introduction of the shared lounge this 'challenging behaviour' greatly reduced. Dan was able to access staff on his terms, choosing when to come and go, allowing him to follow the ebb and flow of his feelings of anxiety and to take some control.

Recognising the possible impact of the décor is also an important aspect of using the PIE principles.

The home should strive for balance between utility and decoration. As a functional space dealing with bodily fluids and high footfall, and working within the bounds of infection control, it must be able to be cleaned easily, and yet these concerns should not take precedence.

The National Specifications for cleaning in care homes states:

> in developing these specifications, regard has been had at all times for the principle of 'proportionality' – which recognises that care homes aim to provide a place where people feel at home and furthermore that in some cases the specific aim will be to support people to be independent in a homely environment, and to have a choice over their daily life. Arrangements to keep the environment clean must therefore take this into account.[13]

It is an unfortunate reality that in traditional institutions the more complex the individuals' needs, the more utilitarian the environment becomes – you only need to enter an acute mental health ward to recognise this. Here, again, we must reflect upon whether this suits the system and management or the client. Working as we do at Highwater House, with tri-morbidity and complex needs, this could lead to an environment which caters predominantly for the most obvious point of need – physical health and the repercussions of addiction (blood, vomit, and so on). An environment focussed principally on these areas will, however, compound the triggers and drivers of the addiction – isolation, rootlessness, and anxiety – reinforcing the need to use substances and creating a vicious cycle. Using the PIE principles ensures we give the emotional wellbeing of the residents' parity when considering the design of the home.

The *2012 Good Practice Guide* highlights areas of the physical environment which have been found to impact on psychological and emotional health. These are:

- Noise and acoustics
- Use of light
- Open green areas
- Art and aesthetics
- Colours[14]

Design for Behavioural and Mental Health: More than just safety (found at healthdesign.org) states that 'certain design features are important for behavioural and mental health treatment facilities/units', and these features are:

- 'A homelike deinstitutionalised environment that supports patient autonomy and control over their environment
- A well maintained, well-organised environment
- Noise control

- Support for privacy
- Support of feelings of personal safety
- Support for social interaction
- Positive distraction.'[15]

The paper *Well-being through design: transferability of design concepts for healthcare environments to ordinary community settings* suggests having 'visually striking objects' to reduce the anxiety of being in a place where people are being asked to face up to the 'challenging content of their experiences'.[16] The paper suggests encouraging users of the environment to adapt their environment – to have easily moveable chairs for example – to enhance their experience of the space they are in and to create a feel of belonging.

The changes we made at Highwater House reflect these suggestions. We have improved our outside space, making it more inviting, and changed the artwork around the home to spark interest in the environment. We have a large centrepiece work of art in our foyer – a colourfully painted four-foot-tall model of a gorilla, one of many sold for charity after being displayed throughout Norwich as part of a community art exhibition – a focal point in an otherwise relatively formal area of the home.

Our aim has been to mindfully deinstitutionalise a setting which has the potential to invoke feelings of submission, indifference, and anxiety. This is a fluid process, and at Highwater House feels quite organic, as we continue to find ways to use the PIE principles to direct us towards a more relaxed and affirming environment.

Workers

Physical changes around the building must be matched by workers' attitude and a thoughtful use of the environment. They must be deliberate in their actions, ensuring they do not compound feelings of distress or apathy in the residents as they share the space.

At Highwater House, workers do not wear uniforms and rarely wear lanyards or ID tags – these being symbolic of power over the environment and residents. Our key card system means there are no bunches of keys being rattled, which had historically been a trigger for residents who have been in prison. Staff used to have a large set of keys, which would get jangled as they were swung about – this had a noticeably negative effect on residents. One used to shout 'here come the screws' when he heard the keys clattering as workers accessed various parts of the building; the sound reminded him of being locked up in his cell in prison and was creating in him a sense that the home was a custodial environment.

As workers complete their tasks around the home, they should use every opportunity to break down traditional roles and enhance their relationships with residents. The mundane and routine actions can be a springboard for conversation about the residents' pasts, or hopes for the future. Thus, the laundry becomes a connection point as a resident shares a memory of hanging out washing with her mother; cleaning the sofa sparks a conversation about searching for money when the electric had run out. In a PIE, workers are promoted to actively follow these stories and to create a narrative arc that frames the resident beyond their diagnosis and assessed needs.

Nutrition

Nothing proves equality more than sitting at a table together and breaking bread: food is a universal need and a great leveller. To give food shows care, to receive food shows acceptance of the community. At Highwater House, workers eat every meal alongside residents – nutrition, and relationships with food, are given particular attention.

Amongst a resident population that has experienced childhood trauma, addiction, and mental ill-health there is certainty that food will play a part in building trusting relationships. Many residents will have negative associations with food after experiencing neglect, or drug and alcohol use has subdued their appetite. Those of our residents who have been street homeless will often try to hoard food, mistrusting the supply; others refuse food, determined to retain some control over their lives.

Herman writes that food is a point of power broking in situations where people have little power[17] and that survivors of abusive family environments report an overwhelming sense of helplessness as 'the exercise of power is arbitrary. Capricious and absolute. Rules are erratic, inconsistent or patently unfair,'[18] she also notes that trauma survivors are particularly vulnerable to revictimisation and that the mental health system can replicate the behaviour of the abusive family.[19]

> *Barry has been deeply affected by a childhood defined by neglect. His memories of being a small child are of feeling desperately hungry, of his needs not being met. He would often only eat once a day, and meals might be only a bag of crisps.*
>
> *Barry's chronic alcohol use stems from this abuse – he self-medicates his anxiety born from years of neglect. He is often incontinent, especially when he is drunk.*
>
> *Not long after he moved in, Barry was sitting at the table at lunch time when it became clear he had wet himself. When he was asked to*

go and wash and change, he became angry, shouting, 'Leave me alone, I just want to finish my food!'

Later, as we talked to Barry and began to build up a picture of his early life it became clear that food was a point of great anxiety for him. He was consistently fearful that he would not have access to food and he would rather sit in urine-soaked trousers than risk his plate being taken away.

The care and catering staff worked together with Barry to help him understand that at Highwater House he would always have food and always be looked after. It was a slow process, but a consistent approach, proved day by day, that he would always have a meal even if he left the dinner table to use the bathroom, eventually worked and Barry began to trust. Getting to know Barry and his life story, and building good relationships with him, enabled staff to reflect on why Barry was behaving aggressively and respond appropriately.

These days Barry often comes in at breakfast time to get some food and leaves it on the table before going and getting his medication. The whole staff team – chefs, domestics and care workers – understand this is because he feels anxious that the kitchen will be closed, that he might not be able to access food. The whole staff team know not to clear his plate of toast away as he'll be back in his own time; and Barry now trusts it will be there when he returns.

How we offer food, and integrate it into the pattern of the day, therefore becomes very important. Using a psychologically informed approach means workers see mealtimes as a potential to connect, and accept that challenging behaviour around food is driven by past experiences. They recognise that (along with medication times and money) mealtimes are a key potential flash point where residents can show some leverage against a perceived all-powerful system, even if that action is self-destructive.

At Highwater House our chefs cook homemade food, three times a day. They are encouraged to make strong bonds with our residents and are an integral part of the care provision. Chefs join the care team meetings and their input is valued. They also receive training on providing care for traumatised people and have supervision where they are guided to talk openly about the connections they make with the clients.

At Highwater House we have created a narrative that giving food is an expression of care with no strings attached. Residents, entrenched in a human services system full of demands and expectations which can create deep feelings of mistrust and paranoia, are used to workers needing something in return for kindness offered (a care plan, signature or blood test, etc.) The act of giving good, fresh food cannot however be misunderstood – it is a clear and simple proof of care, delivered with compassion.

This chapter has reflected KLOES:

E1

- 'The service looks for and encourages the safe use of innovative and pioneering approaches to care and support, and how it is delivered.'

E3

- 'There is a strong emphasis on the importance of eating and drinking well . . . Staff are aware of people's individual preferences and patterns of eating and drinking and there is flexibility when needed or requested.'
- 'Innovative methods and positive staff relationships are used to encourage those who are reluctant or having difficulty in eating and drinking.'

E6

- 'Space is maximised and used creatively to promote independence.'

C1

- 'There is a strong, visible person-centred culture.'

Notes

1 www.merriam-webster.com/dictionary/environment
2 Sourced from https://store.samhsa.gov/system/files/sma14-4884.pdf, 10.
3 Maté, G., *In the Realm of the Hungry Ghosts* (Vermillion, 2018), 299.
4 Robin Johnson, co-author of "Psychologically Informed Services for Homeless People – Good practice guide" 2012 Dept of Communities and Local Gov and developer of http://pielink.net/
5 Keats et al., 2012, 5, sourced from https://eprints.soton.ac.uk/340022/1/Good%2520practice%2520guide%2520-%2520%2520Psychologically%2520informed%2520services%2520for%2520homeless%2520people%2520.pdf
6 Sourced from www2.kobe-u.ac.jp/~alexroni/IPD%202015%20readings/IPD%202015_7/Galtung_Violence,%20Peace,%20and%20Peace%20Research.pdf, 8.
7 Cockersell, P. (Ed.), *Social Exclusion, Compound Trauma and Recovery* (Jessica Kingsley Publishers, 2018), 103.
8 www.homeless.org.uk/sites/default/files/site-attachments/Creating%20a%20Psychologically%20Informed%20Environment%20-%202015.pdf, 11.

9 Torrington, J., *Upgrading Buildings for Older People* (RIBA Enterprises LTD, 2004), 31.
10 Herman, J., *Trauma and Recovery* (Basic Books, 1997), 160.
11 www.cqc.org.uk/sites/default/files/20171020-adult-social-care-kloes-prompts-and-characteristics-final.pdf, 27.
12 W and S Boex, J Housing Care and Support 15.2, found at PIELINK.net
13 www.gov.im/media/1347300/national-specifications-for-cleaning-in-care-homes-oct-14.pdf
14 Keats et al., 2012, 19.
15 www.healthdesign.org/system/files/res_files/Executive%20Summary_Behavioral%20Health_2018.docx.pdf
16 W and S Boex, J Housing Care and Support 15.2, found at PIELINK.net
17 Herman, *Trauma and Recovery*, 79.
18 Herman, *Trauma and Recovery*, 98.
19 Herman, *Trauma and Recovery*, 123.

9 Evidence

In this chapter we will:

- Ask whether assessment is always in the residents' best interests
- See narrative work as style of positive assessment
- Be introduced to the Recovery Star
- Explore how strong relationships can reduce the impact of assessment on residents

Auditing and evidencing are necessities in a residential care home. For a service to thrive it must prove its efficiency to funders, its efficacy to inspectors, and its proficiency to senior management. Paper trails are therefore an undeniable necessity of working in residential care. In the interests of clarity, I will presume that the core audits required to safely run a home, such as fire and medication records, are being undertaken to at least a 'CQC good' and comprehensive level. In this chapter we will explore what we evidence regarding residents, and how we set about doing so. Our aim is to move beyond proving care through quantity of evidence and move towards quality of evidence; and to question how to place equal value on soft and hard outcomes.

What to evidence

Residents' lives are framed through assessments conducted by a variety of human services. As we have explored elsewhere in this book this can mean any number of single-use services needing the resident to be a 'whole' client to them. Drug and alcohol services require the resident to be a recovering addict; mental health services need the resident to be working towards mental stability, and so on. There is a need for a constant flow of information about the resident to fulfil each service's remit and for individual workers to prove their worth. This process can involve a large amount of undue, invasive form filling, and fix the residents in a 'professional patient' role, defining them through risk assessments and failed or reached targets. An outcome of this can be that workers feel unable to carry out care in the face of such administrative burden, and clients in turn see them as uncaring or inaccessible.[1] The service user will have spent many years jumping through multiple hoops, being told they are either a success or failure, depending on the current set of rules, created by the services. Rogers writes that 'moral or diagnostic evaluations' are 'always threatening'.[2]

It is therefore imperative that, as we recognise how wearing taking part in these processes might be, the detrimental impact they might have on the emotional wellbeing of the resident. We must be mindful of what we are asking, and ensure it is absolutely necessary. Overuse of paperwork will create distance between worker and resident; managers would do well to recall the old phrase 'you don't fatten a pig by weighing it'.

External services may only see the resident once every couple of months or even less, and are often looking for notable change or 'improvement' in the resident. As their advocate, it is the PIE worker's job to collate and present change taking place within the whole of the person, rather than one specified area of them. This will help the resident, when attending meetings, to speak fluently about their complete experience as a human; rather than as a fractured set of diagnoses, responding solely through the questioner's lens.

Here, Eddie is in a medication review with a psychiatrist –

> 'So, how are your voices, Eddie?'
> 'Still there, I find them really annoying'
> 'Are you taking your meds?'
> 'Yes, but I find it hard to sleep – I feel agitated'
> Ok. What about drug use?'
> 'Yeah, I'm using a few times a week'

Inevitably the questions are framed around Eddie's mental ill-health and medication needs, a framework which defines him as a mentally unwell drug user. The evidence the psychiatrist collects then supports this view. Despite any best intentions, specialists must have a professional bias through which the resident behaviour is viewed.

Another view of Eddie, from the perspective of the care home PIE worker, is that he is proving himself to be very well mannered and thoughtful, holding the door open for people and on one occasion bringing flowers to the office. He has spent more time in the shared lounge recently and has helped tidy it at the end of the evening. Staff have noticed that he is becoming more comfortable to continue sitting with them when he is responding to his voices, when previously he would feel embarrassed to do so. He has opened conversations up about his past and has shown insight into his drug use – despite it not 'improving'.

We must search for ways to evidence these kind and more human parts of Eddie, as well as cataloguing his distress and illness. To move away from diagnosis towards experience. If we do not do so, we are playing a part in structural violence, containing him in a contaminated identity. At Highwater House we keep a shared lounge diary, filled out at the end of each day. In it we can create a general narrative about the feel of the evening and about any notable 'soft' outcomes – a moment of peer support, of a positive group dynamic, or, as above, someone helping to tidy up. Across a period of months this diary shows broader ebbs and flows of the social fabric of the home, and can help pick out individual residents' growth as well. This diary is also a key source of our statistics, helping us to log moments of connection with our residents.

Narrative work

Much of our work in a PIE involves supporting residents to re-frame their experience as they choose, using their own words. As we spend quality time with our clients and forge strong bonds, we can support them to tease out strands of their lives which are not bound by the needs of the helping services. They can paint a picture of their lives where they are not defined by mental illness, rather, by their hobbies or future hopes. Narrative therapy calls these 'sparkling moments' – a time when a person's story is not dominated by a central narrative arc of problems, but of hope and change. We can help residents find these moments by remaining aware of our own language, especially as we collect information or evidence.

Using a trauma-informed approach, we can:

- Recognise the resident is the expert on themselves
- Use open-ended questions
- Frame questions by positively asking 'what has happened?' not 'what is wrong?'
- Recognise that asking for information might be retraumatising

We have a duty to record information about all aspects of the resident, positive as well as negative. It is all too easy to log what is wrong, rather than what is right. The narrative approach helps us to remain strengths-based in our evidence collection and daily logs, alongside the need to record risk, issues, or problems.

The mental health recovery star

Creating a Psychologically Informed Environment states 'PIEs aim to bring about behavioural change. These can be small but significant and if not identified and monitored they may be overlooked.'[3]

At Highwater House we use the Mental Health Recovery Star to help us track progress.

Separated into ten areas, the star asks residents to grade themselves in each area on a scale between one and ten. This approach reflects a common framework used in solution-focussed brief therapy. The ten areas are:

- Managing mental health
- Self-care
- Living skills
- Social networks
- Work
- Relationships
- Addictive behaviour
- Responsibilities
- Identity and self-esteem
- Trust and hope[4]

We can see that many of these areas focus on soft skills and personal growth rather than hard skills such as budgeting. This tool may not be suitable for all residents, and at Highwater House there are no demands that they take part. However, when the time is right, the star can help residents to create a visual narrative of success. For example, they may be able to move up the scale if they have shown interest in their personal hygiene, or taken some responsibility for an aggressive outburst, if they have an improved appetite or accepted a cup of tea and sat down for a few minutes in the lounge. The changes may be slight, but should be registered and applauded.

Time-outs, evictions, emergency services, and meaningful contact

At Highwater House we are obligated to gather statistics to prove the service's efficacy to commissioners. This process has given us the opportunity to show a snapshot of before and after we introduced the PIE approach in the home. Whilst they are used elsewhere in this book it is, I believe, worth revisiting such a notable set of results (Under-1-Roof is a training and development centre next door to Highwater House, and part of St Martins). Highwater began to use the PIE principles in 2017.

Event	2016	2017	2018	2019
2-hour time-out	104	68	60	48
24-hour time-out	7	2	2	2
Police called by staff	28	14	2	3
Untoward incident	67	53	20	18
On-site activity	560	959	2293	2662
Under-1-Roof activity	48	288	383	380
Total activities	918	1658	3059	3430

These statistics prove that creating a service focussed on improving rapport and building bonds can have far-reaching consequences, including a reduction of conflict and use of emergency services. Most importantly, for the residents it means the home has become a calmer space with greater potential to connect with fellow humans; using the PIE principles has unlocked that potential.

Anecdotal evidence

Working closely with people means sharing their stories, and it is through anecdotes that our work can often be best shown. Personal stories create and hold a community together, and workers can use them to strengthen a narrative of warmth, acceptance, and, even when there seems little to celebrate, success.

> Sandra came to Highwater House as an unkempt lady in her late forties. She had been through a period of psychosis and, as she had been detained under the Mental Health Act for some time, had lost the tenancy on her flat. As her psychosis took hold, her relationship with her daughter and grandchildren had broken down. Her poor mental health had led her to gouging holes into the walls of her flat because she thought there were dead bodies behind them; she was leaving her home wearing only a nightgown and walking down the street, vulnerable and talking to herself. Neighbours were concerned by her erratic behaviour and contacted mental health services.
>
> Sandra soon settled at Highwater; she quickly fell into a positive pattern of eating well, sleeping well, and accepting help with personal care. She was on a low, holding methadone script and was concordant with her mental health medication. Over the course of ten months she stabilised and was able to restart a relationship with her family which she was delighted about.
>
> Sadly, Sandra was found dead in her bathroom at the home. She had injected herself with heroin and had bought morphine off the street. She

> *had overdosed in the night. She had just returned from a week away with her family and had been buoyant about her future plans to move on into a flat again.*

Sandra's story is of course sad, but it is not solely negative. She was well-clothed and clean, felt supported and had built trusting relationships with workers and other residents. She had become very much herself again; not a mentally ill person shuffling down the street semi-naked, distressed, and scared, but a mother and grandmother, a woman who had strong opinions and enjoyed laughing. She was the protagonist of a positive narrative shaped with the help of the environment and staff and, despite her untimely death, can be seen by the service as a success.

Sandra, then, could simply be another negative statistic – a heroin overdose – or she can be celebrated as an engaged individual who was being supported to make the best of what she had. I believe the second version of Sandra is a more genuine, honest one; and one that comes closer to honouring her as a person. It also gives the staff credit for the reparative work they did with her, and provides comfort to other residents. Using case studies like Sandra's gives staff the chance to reflect on their work – on the elements of Sandra's care which worked well – and provides a chance to see success where cold statistics show failure. It allows the staff to frame such events with realism and helps promote the continuation of their good work.

Assessment

Sourcing evidence need not involve sitting down opposite a resident and asking them questions. Doing so will enforce the differing roles that workers and residents have and will erode trust, reinforcing the resident in their 'patient' role. PIE workers who spend as much time connecting authentically with the residents as possible have the opportunity to undertake silent assessments without the resident knowing.

> *Matt suffers from paranoid schizophrenia, and has been in the system for many years. He does not trust health workers and views any mention of appointments with suspicion. He refuses to be seen by doctors and finds questions about his health invasive. Due to a chronic illness he has twice become affected by gangrene, leading to partial amputation of digits. Staff need to regularly check his hands for any signs of gangrene returning.*
>
> *If a staff member asks him to show them his hands he refuses, putting his hands in his pockets and walking away.*
>
> *Matt has a good rapport with some workers, who have persevered and built good relationships with him. In the morning he'll shake hands*

with them, he'll accept cups of tea and medication, and sit at the dinner table and eat with them.

At no point is a hand check mentioned, however staff have, throughout the day, been able to unobtrusively monitor his health, physically checking and looking at his hands for any signs of infection.

There are many situations where, using the PIE principle of sharing space, workers can reduce mechanical or institutionalised care. Sitting next to a resident on the sofa to watch the soaps is an opportunity to check their temperature, sharing a cup of tea lets the worker monitor a resident's hands.

In Matt's case, shaking hands each morning is a sign of inclusion, and, surreptitious checks or not, builds trust. If workers insisted he show them his hands, much of the reparative work done over many months would be lost, the power dynamic becoming acutely obvious, with a certainty that his counterwill would be triggered.

Our job in a PIE is to remain aware of how our actions affect others, and to accept that their response to us is affected by a lifetime of experiences. When collecting evidence, we must remain mindful that undue levels of paperwork will create stress and could compound feelings of anxiety and powerlessness. As we ask residents to share their life stories, we must accept that they are, in effect, using their past trauma as currency to procure shelter, support, and care. Recognising this means the PIE worker can try, as far as possible, to soften the edges of the system and reduce the impact upon the resident. By doing so they will achieve a much greater outcome than a series of statistics, they will take part in congruent human connection.

This chapter has reflected KLOES:

S1

- 'The service is particularly creative in the way it involves and works with people to understand their diverse circumstances and individual needs.'

S2

- 'There is a transparent and open culture that encourages creative thinking in relation to people's safety.'

C1

- 'There is a strong, visible person-centred culture.'

Notes

1 Daley, A., Costa, L. and Beresford, P. (Eds.), *Madness, Violence, and Power* (University of Toronto Press, 2019), 270.
2 Rogers, C. R., *On Becoming a Person* (Constable, 2004), 34.
3 www.homeless.org.uk/sites/default/files/site-attachments/Creating%20a%20Psychologically%20Informed%20Environment%20-%202015.pdf, 15.
4 Sourced from https://midpowysmind.org.uk/wp-content/uploads/2018/06/Recovery-STAR-User-Guide.pdf

10 Rules, roles, and responsiveness (the 3 Rs)

In this chapter we will:

- Explore using rules as guiding principles to improve workers' engagement with residents
- See roles can be positive or negative, depending on how they are used
- See the recruitment process as key to promoting Trauma-Informed Care
- Find that the whole organisation should use PIE principles and be trauma-informed

Pielink.net explains the '3 Rs' as 'essential ingredients . . . that focus on immediate and practical expressions of the way a service works' – taken together rules, roles, and responsiveness place 'emphasis on practical and organisational issues, in a services day-to-day dealings, especially with clients (but also with its own staff and other agencies)'.[1]

The 3 Rs, then, are concerned with the social life, or social structure of the service – they are, essentially, a way of defining the 'whole home' ecology, or service culture. This area of a PIE will be evidenced through the language that workers use, and their behaviour around the service. The 3 Rs are tools managers and workers can use to frame their best practice and as reflective points as they move through their day.

Introduced in the PIE 2.0 formula, this element reflects an important aspect of the KLOES – that a service is Well-led and Effective. Providing long-term care can create the conditions where carers stop being aware of their impact upon the residents and unintentionally harm them. Kitwood used the term malignant social psychology to describe this state where the residents' personhood is eroded. The 3 Rs help residential care workers remain aware of the impact their systems might have on their residents.

Rules

Using the PIE approach necessitates a shift towards a more person-centred service culture, and asks for improved staff awareness around their actions and impact upon the environment. The systems we use will need to be redefined, moving away from a task-orientated, 'action equals achievement' culture, and towards one where workers take increasingly personal responsibility for their conduct as the primary goal. The language we use in our daily work shapes the way we see and experience events; and so, the way rules are worded is critical, especially when working with survivors of trauma, or those with complex needs.

As we have explored in previous chapters, simplifying the rules down to key, easily understood messages helps residents to live successfully within the care home environment. At Highwater House our two day-to-day rules are:

- No violence to people or property
- No drugs on the premises

Beyond these, workers are promoted to work within the 'grey area' of embodying boundaries and to use prosocial behaviour modelling, which ultimately helps the residents take ownership over their own actions (remember, trauma creates helplessness and recovery is based on empowerment).

Workers, then, need guiding principles to help them negotiate this shared grey area.

Our guiding principles at Highwater House reflect the three stages of trauma recovery, and are a reflective framework within which staff should always work. These are:

- Safety
- Acceptance
- Inclusivity

In the trauma-informed model, the first stage of recovery is for the survivor to become safe,[2] the second, for them to tell their story,[3] and the third is for them to reconnect with the community.[4]

Utilising these rules, or principles, ensures the worker is not further traumatising the client, and is supporting them to enact positive change through their interactions.

Verbalising these rules around the home also assists the resident peer group as they bear witness to one another's stories. Used consistently, they direct everybody within the home to respond to each other's needs with compassion. Adopting first person plural personal pronouns – we, our, us, or ourselves – helps to create belonging within the home's community, for example, 'We don't fight in here, we give people space if they need it', or 'Why don't we try to find a way through this?'

Each resident, as they go through the process of entering the home and settling into the community, will be at different stages of the trauma recovery cycle. Thus, one resident might be in chronic need of physical care as they experience the full force of their addiction (they might return to the home a number of times a day, drenched in urine, or covered in vomit; or walk round the home shouting and being physically challenging), whilst another needs emotional support and a listening ear as they practice being accepted into a community. Inevitably, this can lead to friction. These shared rules, instilled through regular use of supportive language, help to create a common voice within the home of altruism, acceptance, and respect.

Values

As workers use these rules, they should also exemplify shared values which are solution focussed and accessible; these values add to the culture of acceptance and inclusivity in the home, and are protective of our vulnerable clients. Again, they can be verbalised throughout the working day as guiding principles to counsel staff and residents.

At Highwater House, and across the entire St Martins family, our values are to be:

- Nurturing
- Tenacious
- Open
- Progressive

These values are in keeping with our overarching framework, explored in the chapter on psychological awareness, of kindness, empathy, and emotional literacy, and promote outward-looking care; and a determination to provide for others even in the face of great challenge.

It might be that a set of values can best be verbalised in more readily accessible language; for example, Mahatma Ghandi said 'Be the change you wish to see in the world'. This is a value-based statement – clear, positive, grounded in personal action, and inclusive.

108 *Rules, roles, and responsiveness*

The rules of the home define the *feel* of the home, and it is that feel that visitors, residents, and workers will respond to.

Roles

The roles available around the home impact the feel of the home. Much of this book is an exploration into the impact that living within a powerful system can have upon a service user, and how staff should remain acutely aware of how powerful, and authoritarian, their roles can be (or seem to others). Workers gateway warmth, shelter and food as well as friendship, connection and support. If workers do not fully reflect upon their status and influence, they may increase the residents' psychological and emotional pain. The 'Senior' who's 'in charge today', for example, automatically places themselves in the role of rule-maker, whilst use of 'expert' language by staff infers we have 'inexpert' residents. In a PIE care home, our goal is for workers to become the professional family – to reduce jargon and increase accessibility.

The role of the service user is often defined through passive or impotent language. The helped, ill, abused, or in need. If they try to exert strength against the system, their actions are defined through risk, and not welcomed as an expression of selfhood.

Working in a PIE care home, we take every opportunity to remove our professional 'hats'. By integrating themselves into a peer support role – shown physically through sharing meals, sharing lounges, and removing themselves from points of authority around the building such as offices – workers become facilitators of recovery, rather than controllers of recovery,[5] and there is a natural flattening of the power structure felt within the home. Managers are included in this process, and should strive to create a feeling of mutuality amongst themselves, residents, and staff.

Making effort to share ownership of the space cultivates self-advocacy within the clients, and helps to reduce any sense of coercion. Creating collaborative roles, however minor, will lead to stronger relationships, and improve wellbeing in the resident. Every member of the care team can play a part in this – at Highwater House the maintenance man will take time to listen, and find ways to incorporate an eager resident into his day (usually by listening to stories of past DIY successes or failures).

Roles should be made available within the home that can be applied to anyone and everyone – reducing exclusivity improves feelings of inclusivity. These roles should be couched in accessible, emotional terms – roles of compassion, care, support, and kindness. These can then be attributed to anybody, resident or worker, who fulfils that role and so becomes a success. A resident who supports another resident should be rewarded with recognition of that compassion (being given a compassionate role), in the same way a worker might. This helps create an environment based on empowerment, and is a unifying process.

Recruitment

The PIE principles can be further embedded into the service culture through improved recruitment practice. Interview questions can be changed to incorporate psychologically informed practice and and altered to best uncover the soft skills of kindness, empathy, and resilience. Whilst a training programme can teach anybody about the Mental Health Act, Manual Handling or Mental Capacity, it is vastly more difficult to train a person to have authentic empathy for a client, or to be truly kind.

In a PIE interview then, we are assessing an ability and willingness to connect with residents, and an awareness of the trauma-informed approach. The traditional interview process can be a stilted dance of professionalism with the interviewer and interviewee playing out roles without sharing much emotional content. Here, we are breaking this down by finding ways for the interviewee to express themselves more freely.

The National Council for Behavioural Health provides a non-exhaustive list of sample trauma-informed interview questions. Here I have taken some example questions that are particularly useful for a PIE care home. The wording used in the questions elicit emotional language in the response.

- What techniques have you found to be effective in developing trusting relationships and rapport with clients?
- Tell us about a time you were sensitive or compassionate to a client in an emotional or tense situation
- Collaborative work often eases tension and facilitates productive relationships. Can you give an example of where you intentionally enhanced a relationship to achieve a goal?
- Provide an example of how you monitored/managed morale and health of your co-workers to help them work to their potential
- Tell me about a time you became overwhelmed with your work. What were the signs and how did you resolve the situation?[6]

Embedding the PIE principles begins through the recruitment process, and is then continued through training and development.

The role of the service

The principles of PIE and Trauma-Informed Care should be integrated throughout the entire structure of an organisation. It is important that the system responds in a trauma-informed way, as well as the individual worker. As we have previously seen, and will explore further in the next chapter, every member of staff on the frontline should be supported to have improved psychological awareness, and of trauma-informed practice. This, then, is also true for senior managers, policy-makers, and directors. The feel of the entire organisation should be attuned to the needs of the traumatised clients, with a shared understanding of how the experience of traumatic events impact everybody involved.

> The program, organisation, or system responds by applying the principles of a trauma-informed approach to all areas of functioning. The program, organisation, or system integrates an understanding that the experience of traumatic events impacts all people involved, whether directly or indirectly. Staff in every part of the organisation, from the person who greets clients at the door to the executives and governance board, have changed their language, behaviours and policies to take into consideration the experiences of trauma among children and adult service users of the services and among staff providing the services.[7]

This roots to branches, collective awareness of trauma-informed practice ensures the system is actively resisting trauma and reducing the risk of retraumatising the service user as they access different parts of the organisation. Herman writes: 'to hold traumatic reality in consciousness requires a social context that affirms and protects the victims ... for the larger society the social context is created by political movements that give voice to the disempowered'.[8] For every part of the organisation to use the PIE principles and have understanding of trauma-informed principles places the residents' experiences within a greater social context, and so allows them to engage in the healing process. The duty of the organisation, as an enveloping social system, is to work holistically with the service user.

Highwater House has become a driving force in rolling out the PIE principles across the St Martins family of services. Using the PIE approach is helping to create a shared language, and to instil trauma-informed practice across the organisation, and this remains an ongoing process.

Responsiveness

How we respond (or are perceived to respond) to events within the home and as a wider organisation creates a narrative that stretches far beyond our front door. How the service is known to other professional bodies is an important aspect of running a successful home. Therefore, the service must avoid being seen as faceless, inaccessible, or of perpetuating structural violence. The residents' stories *are* the home's story. The mental health wards in Britain, for example, struggle to avoid being seen as a coercive system, where patients doubt the sincerity of claims to care.[9] The negative personal narratives of the service user affects the whole system. The domino effect of this is that *all* of the mental health system is often seen in the same light. Having strong, value-based statements about the intent of the home, and the qualities the service wishes to embody helps to frame it as a progressive, responsive, and accessible partner in the clients' care.

Transition

Moving through the stages of trauma recovery ultimately leads to greater stability in the residents' lives. To do so successfully means processing through different roles within the home – this should be encouraged by the workers. A resident might start out in the role of rebel or agitator, challenging the system, or as disinterested observer, unwilling or unable to connect. Over time they might use the roles of brother, friend, or supporter as they begin to test the relationship and to integrate their experience of trauma into their narrative. As they reach a point where they can sustain personal equilibrium without excessive substance use, they may want to move on from the service. This stage of recovery can be fraught with indecision and worry, which must be framed as a natural response to an unsettling process.

Funding models create a strict distinction between services – when residents leave one, they are expected to neatly move not only their physical belongings but also their emotional connections to the other. They meet a new key worker and a new peer group. The old safe service becomes an inaccessible past whilst the new service is an unknown, uncertain future. The resident is asked to trust this leap into no-man's land with eagerness, yet the process can be destabilising, the secure base, painstakingly created, shaken. To help the resident succeed in this transition the service should find creative ways to remain porous – welcoming back residents and integrating their move into the narrative of the home. Just as the Cycle of Change allows for relapse in recovery, the workers in a PIE care home should be ready for the return of ex-residents. If they arrive at the door it will be purposeful – possibly a need to briefly reconnect with a secure space.

Survivors of trauma will experience returns of traumatic memory, or have moments where they do not feel that they can cope. This might be due to a significant reminder of the trauma, or a change in life circumstances. Returning to a secure base where they know they have been accepted will help them continue their journey of integrating the traumatic experience into their personal history.[10]

At Highwater House we have created a 'parachute period' where residents are welcome back to the home for meals and to socialise; their key workers will visit in their new homes and the new key workers are invited to come to Highwater in the run up to the resident's move. This helps soften the process of leaving, and assures the resident that their needs will be met. There is a joint projection of success by all involved. Over time, Highwater House's key worker will reduce involvement in a considered decrescendo of care, mindfully moving the support package away from them. The ideal outcome is for the resident to reject them – saying they no longer need the worker to pop by. Trauma recovery is based on empowerment, and this symbolises their power over their situation.

Managers

Managers are responsible for the feel of the service and are the primary motivating force for change. How they respond to events around the home sets the tone for others. The PIE principles are a tool managers can use to instil a person-centred culture which gives parity to the emotional aspects of the residents' care – if they are seen to focus solely on targets, enforcement, and monitoring, or are risk averse, the staff will inevitably follow suit. If, however, the manager proves they tolerate uncertainty, can engage with 'unreachable' clients, and can successfully operate in the grey areas of behaviour management, then workers will feel supported to do so as well.

Carers will, of course, see themselves as kind, compassionate and empathetic, meaning the culture of the care home is based on valuing emotional responses; and yet these values can be overshadowed by routine task-orientated behaviour. The PIE principles can be key to converting these caring values into action. Making the residents' 'psychological make-up – the thinking, emotions, personalities and past experience'[11] – the guiding force in our care provision places greater emphasis on the residents' story as a whole person, rather than focussing on their physical health needs or mental health diagnosis.

Public narrative (Ganz 2010) recognises that 'the key to motivation is understanding that values inspire action through emotion'.[12] Managers, then, can use their public narrative, their value-based psychologically informed storytelling, to elicit an emotional, and therefore motivated, response in workers. The manager's narrative of placing value upon the day-to-day, impromptu interactions between workers and residents gives those connections a quality which can be celebrated.

The 3 Rs – taken together – express the collective narrative of the home, the stories of managers, staff, and residents. It is not only for individuals that we should search for narrative theory's 'sparkling moments', but for the service as well.

The PIE principles help to create a public narrative based on values, quality care, hope and personal achievement, which will seep into the culture of the organisation. As a psychologically informed language becomes embedded, this person-centred culture will self-seed, spread throughout the resident population, and permeate the policies, procedures, and day-to-day running of the home.

This chapter has reflected KLOES:

E4

- 'There is a thorough approach to planning and coordinating people's move to other services.'

C1

- 'Staff demonstrate a real empathy for the people they care for.'

W1

- 'Staff are motivated by, and proud of the service.'

Notes

1 http://pielink.net/the-three-rs/
2 Herman, J., *Trauma and Recovery* (Basic Books, 1997), 160.
3 Herman, *Trauma and Recovery*, 174.
4 Herman, *Trauma and Recovery*, 196.
5 SAMHSA's 'Concept of Trauma and Guidance for a Trauma-Informed Approach' sourced from https://s3.amazonaws.com/static.nicic.gov/Library/028436.pdf, 11.
6 Sourced from www.nationalcouncildocs.net/wp-content/uploads/2014/01/Interview-Questions-for-Trauma-Informed-Care.pdf
7 SAMHSA's 'Concept of Trauma and Guidance for a Trauma-Informed Approach'.
8 Herman, *Trauma and Recovery*, 9.
9 Daley, A., Costa, L. and Beresford, P. (Eds.), *Madness, Violence, and Power* (University of Toronto Press, 2019), 270.
10 Herman, *Trauma and Recovery*, 174.
11 Robin Johnson, co-author of 'psychologically informed services for homeless people' good practice guide 2012. department of communities and local gov. and developer of pielink.net
12 Found at www.ndi.org/sites/default/files/Public%20Narrative%20Participant%20Guide.pdf

11 Staff support and training

In this chapter we will:

- See training is key to implementing the PIE approach
- Explore support and supervision as a reflective and supportive process
- See supervision as an opportunity to introduce and embed the PIE principles
- Be introduced to compassion fatigue and vicarious trauma, and explore them as debilitating conditions for the carer

Staff training and supervision should be an enabling process: protective, engaging, and proactive. With suitable training workers will feel confident in their work in a PIE whilst robust support will help alleviate any difficulties that arise.

Using the PIE principles in a registered care home means looking beyond the common mandatory training regime, and introducing at least basic understanding of psychological theory, talking therapies, and emotional literacy. It is presumed throughout this chapter that all mandatory training has been completed, and so will focus on additional PIE training. In the interests of clarity, a typical core training programme will include:

- Health and Safety
- Fire Safety
- Equality, Diversity and Human Rights
- Infection, Prevention and Control
- Manual Handling
- Food Hygiene/Food Safety Awareness
- Safeguarding Adults[1]

As we have discovered in the chapter on psychological awareness, our aim is to use our improved psychological knowledge to support the staff team to remain kind and empathetic in the face of challenging behaviour, and to provide consistent care to survivors of trauma who struggle to accept support.

Regulation 18 of the Health and Social Care Act states: 'Staff must receive the support, training, professional development, supervision and appraisals that are necessary for them to carry out their role and responsibilities.'[2] Introducing the PIE principles into a service, and changing the remit to give parity to emotional health, leads us to see this regulation in a new light. Equally, recognising that survivors of trauma, or those who have been negatively affected by the mental health system, might feel emotionally unsafe means we should see the CQC's fundamental standard on safety – that 'providers must assess the risks to your health and safety during any care or treatment and make sure their staff have the qualifications, competence, skills and experience to keep you safe'[3] – in terms of psychological and emotional safety. In a PIE our responsibilities have a new focus on psychological wellbeing, and our training and development of staff must reflect this.

Training

Introducing new ways of working into a service will almost certainly lead to some resistance from workers: 'if it ain't broke, don't fix it', 'what's the point', 'it's just another management thing'. Some staff at Highwater House were concerned how the residents might react if we upset the equilibrium of the home, worrying they might 'vote with their feet'. Others felt that the service would lose a certain uniqueness if change were forced upon it – a long-serving senior project worker at Highwater House was concerned we 'might lose our magic' by introducing a new style of care. He is, now, a leading proponent of the PIE ethos within the team – 'why didn't we do this sooner – it's so obvious'.

The manager's job then is to create a 'whole home' buy-in; to promote the PIE initiative as an enhancement and celebration of the team's best work; and to implement it across the entire strata of the workforce – from domestic workers to senior managers. The aim is to create a tipping point where the number of psychologically informed practices around the home encompass the whole home ecology – this will be shown through workers' attitude, behaviour, and language. This will, then, with careful curation, become self-sustaining. Gladwell describes the tipping point as the 'moment of critical mass, the threshold, the boiling point',[4] and that involving the whole home in creating a shared PIE language of compassion, kindness, and understanding means this point will be reached with enthusiasm for the process. Here, the actions of a domestic worker catching a reticent resident for a game of cards and a brief, friendly chat carries as much weight as a twelve-page assessment carried out by care workers; the intention and intuition of their actions are recognised and lauded; and the PIE model is in place.

Cockersell writes: 'It makes sense for the whole staff team, including management, to undergo training in the PIE approach together . . . Training should not be only for frontline staff: it is important that middle and senior management have some training in PIE too.'[5] *Creating a Psychologically Informed Environment* states services should 'create a core training program which supports the implementation of psychologically informed practice. All staff (catering, maintenance, cleaning and security etc.), and volunteers, attend to support shared understanding.'[6]

At Highwater House, as explored in the chapter on Psychological Awareness, we introduced training on PIE, Trauma-Informed Care, and Dialectical Behavioural Therapy, as well as staff having prior training in a host of other therapeutic interventions. Whilst some of the training gained more traction (Trauma-Informed Care) than others (DBT), the key outcomes were creating an interest in the PIE model, and embedding a narrative arc that change, though worrying, could be a positive thing. Using this training we could begin to envisage a roadmap of how we wanted the service to look and, importantly, *feel* as a PIE, and gain guidance as we started to enact change on the ground.

Training, along with supervision and support, helped considerably to allay the staff team's fears that this new way of working would overshadow their already excellent approach to care provision. The training showed the PIE model to be a supportive framework, one which would complement and augment their best practice; and one which would assist, rather than hinder, the team to further their work. This has then been compounded in the reality of working as a PIE, and the provable, excellent, outcomes we have achieved – shown through statistics and anecdotes.

Our experience of becoming a PIE at Highwater House has been an organic, gradual process – and one which will continue for many years to come. Trying to introduce lots of new theory and practice into a workplace is fraught with difficulty. It is, inevitably, a process of trial and error, of missteps and successes.

If it is training and progressive management which lays the foundations, then it is the whole staff team who build the structure, adding idiosyncratic ideas and their unique perspective throughout the services adaption.

Support and supervision

Empathy is the carer's primary tool, and should be celebrated, honed, and supported. A carer's empathy is not a bottomless well, therefore carers must be purposefully supported by robust supervision, just as they support residents.

This element of the PIE framework is already a legislative requirement in care homes, and is part of the CQC's expectation of continuous development and improvement. Therefore, rather than exploring the need for managerial and clinical supervision, focus will be upon quality and the style of supervision best suited for working as a PIE. The Health and Social Care Act states: 'staff must receive the support, training, professional development, supervision and appraisals that are necessary for them to carry out their role and responsibilities', and we know that 'the consequences of absent, inadequate, or negative forms of supervision constitute a major threat to workforce stability, capacity, confidence, competence and morale'.[7]

The paper, *Supervision Now or Never*, explores what supervision should *not* be. It states,

> supervision is not practice audit. The focus on performance management has come to dominate the process. Supervisors report that they are expected to use supervision to audit adherence to processes leaving little time to explore the quality of assessment decision making and intervention. Workers frequently report. . . . the priority becomes compliance checking rather than exploration of practice.[8]

In the busy care home, it may be all too easy for supervision to become a box-ticking exercise, a routine experience to ensure a paper trail for the CQC. The PIE framework, placing focus on Trauma-Informed Care and reflective practice, helps frame supervisions as a space where workers are encouraged to explore their relationships with residents, and to flag concerns before they become problematic.

Creating a Psychologically Informed Environment, regarding supervision, advises:

- 'Management take an active role in supporting and promoting the health and wellbeing of their staff
- Acknowledge the emotional demands of working with individuals who have complex needs and have a discussion to identify how to minimise any negative impact
- Have an "open-door" approach
- There are debriefs after an incident, difficult conversation or shift
- The service culture supports staff to talk openly about how their work is making them feel.
- Provide access to an employee assistance programme
- Supervision includes an element of reflection

118 *Staff support and training*

- Internal or specialist staff provide support to staff and clients e.g. psychologists facilitate reflective practice and provide counselling or group work for clients
- Ask for regular feedback on staff health and wellbeing, or their attitudes and beliefs about work.'[9]

At Highwater House we have managers on the floor, and an open-door policy at all times. This policy is important in an environment where residents living with addiction and deep emotional and chronic physical health issues can have sudden and disastrous episodes with dire consequences. The importance of access to an immediate and comprehensive debrief in these situations cannot be overstated; supporting the worker to reflect on their actions and thoughts in a given situation can mean the difference between a worker taking long-term sick leave or accepting and learning from an event.

At Highwater there are clear lines of accountability, and workers are promoted to openly and honestly explore any issues they may have with residents. We recognise that carers are human, and that breaking down traditional roles, as we are asking them to in a PIE, could leave staff feeling vulnerable as they leave the safety of their more conventional carers role. A central premise of the PIE initiative is that staff are accessible to residents, with fewer boundaries between them – this, then, must also be true for staff with managers.

A common proposal throughout most literature about PIEs is that workers should have regular access to a psychologist who can guide and support staff in their work. This is, though, an initiative which has largely been used in homeless services and hostels. Residents in care will likely already have access to psychiatrists and other health services, with a strong dialogue between psychiatric services and care workers in place – indeed much of this book is about reducing the corrosive impact that long-term contact with helping services can have upon residents, and breaking down the 'professional patient' role. That is not to say that having a psychologist's input would not be valuable, however, the realities of funding models and time-poor mental health services makes this unlikely to happen. Certainly, this is true at Highwater House.

In most care settings it will fall to the supervisor or manager to introduce reflective practice, promote psychological knowledge, and to guide staff through challenging moments. However, becoming a PIE is a fluid process and so, over the coming years at Highwater House we will explore this area further, potentially working with psychology students in the local university, or sourcing funding so far untapped.

In conversation

I've asked two long-standing team members, Eugene and Ross, for feedback on using the PIE model. Below is a transcript of our conversation.

I: How have the using PIE principles affected the home?
E: I would say a lot of the processes are out there already, it's just about pulling them all together – having a structure for it. I think a lot of the boundaries are gone, it's more like a family now. It goes without saying that you have to have a staff team where nearly the whole lot are signed up to the idea of it though. I was very critical at first when it came out but then when I realised it's a lot of what we do anyway it's making more sense, you know?
R: I think, in terms of the way staff interact with people hasn't changed much, I think it was in place here anyway. We have always had a positive and welcoming, responsive attitude – we were never too strict, and judging by what people say about other services, we still aren't.
I: So the staff's way of behaving was already in place?
E: Yeah, but the old model meant our time had to be shared out more, when we were in the office, there were always some people who would join us, they'd have sole attention of us . . . and that would mean others didn't. This way that's not so much of a problem . . .
I: What were your worries, if any?
E: I was worried about having the office open all the time. [this was considered at one point] I didn't think it wouldn't be practical because of the medications and files . . . but then we haven't done that, we've got staff to leave the office, not the other way around, you need some official space . . .
R: Yeah, we're a registered care home . . .
E: Well it might work, we don't know, but I think it's better having staff out and about and . . .
R: When this was first touted it was obvious that staff get as institutionalised as residents . . . but it's relaxed the staff – getting out of the office . . . not waiting for the next fight . . .
E: Well, it's made it more stable . . . a lot of people might be frightened of the term though . . .
I: What are the best aspects of using the PIE model?
E: In the old model there'd be people you would rarely see . . .
I: So it helps to connect with people you might not have seen so much of?
R: I think we can take this further though, finding ways to share space without being too intrusive . . .

120 Staff support and training

I: So has the environment noticeably changed to get people to engage more?
R: Yes.
E: There's been less problems since we started the PIE stuff . . .
R: But is it just luck we have good residents in at the moment though?
E: Well, we've got Phil in recently, he's getting his head round the fact it's not as institutionalised.
R: Funnily enough what Emma [a worker who knew Phil from a different service] says about Phil is he was always getting warnings there . . . but here he seems. . . . Ok . . .
E: It defuses a lot . . . the difficult ones that come in and scowl. Thinking about Sam – he used to come in and sit on his own and look like he wanted to kick off but he questioned himself . . . so he did see the family atmosphere and stop himself . . .
E: It used to be that things would happen between six and ten, but now there's no doors to kick, we're just in the lounge. Last night Carl and Donald were having an argument in there and I could just sit and make sure it didn't go too far . . . Phil was sitting and watching, it all just simmered down . . .
I: To me that's the biggest change . . . the lack of doors . . .
R: Yeah – we were always waiting for something to happen . . .
R: And people were looking for an audience . . .
E: My stress levels have gone right down . . .
R: It's a good place to work, and a good place to live . . . I know that's a bit woolly, but . . . we're looking for human to human work. . . .
E: When they first move in, they can't believe how relaxed I am in the lounge . . .
R: Yeah, it's the expectation that goes two ways, show people how we want other people to behave.
I: Can you think of any particular problems?
R: I do wonder whether there's a gap between the theory . . . and . . . doing it on the ground, as a modus operandi for the staff . . .
R: But then I wonder if TIC and PIE ethos thinking, if it seeps into people's heads without them realising. . . . And, it's all in its infancy . . . the sharing . . . the staff were hesitant. . . .
E: We need a stimulus to keep the momentum . . .
R: The litmus test is how are people when they arrive and how are they when they leave? I hope the interactions are beneficial for when they leave here . . .
I: So they can live successfully elsewhere?
R: Yeah, we need a continuum outside of here . . . they might leave expecting this level of support elsewhere . . . we should ask other services what they think. . . . We can do good work here, but when Glen, for

example, moves on, will he be able to take it with him? I'd like to think so. . . . That the interactions with us all will permeate into him, so when he goes down the local shop, he'll talk to the guys there. PIE is like the glue, the day-to-day conversation.

I: If there was a take home message, what would it be?
E: There are two messages – give it a try, it can't hurt, and to the ones that are already doing it, it's a celebration – there are lots of people out there already doing it, it's giving it a name.
I: And if you had to sum up PIE in fewer than five words?
R: Inclusive, positive.
E: Less them and us.

Introducing PIE through supervision

Supervision is an excellent opportunity to instil psychologically informed themes into the staff team, and to explore any doubts about the approach. Reciprocal determinism shows that behaviour will be followed, especially that of a high-status individual. Managers' behaviour, the way they act and the language they use, will have a ripple effect throughout the fabric of the home. Supervision is a perfect time for managers to embody the message of being psychologically informed.

When introducing the PIE principles to the team at Highwater, supervision gave us a chance to choose common narrative threads to introduce through each staff member's session. These themes supported wider conversation sparked around the home about how to provide best care. And so, during one supervision cycle we incorporated attachment theory; the next, structural violence and power dynamics; and so on. This helped to introduce therapeutic language into the wider vernacular of the home. This continues to be an ongoing process.

Introducing themes in this way allows the supervisor to adapt the style and substance of the conversation to suit each individual worker. It may not be feasible or desirable for every member of staff in the care home to have in-depth knowledge of therapeutic interventions, or to attend lengthy training. A brief overview of a therapeutic concept is however always possible, using examples and case studies from around the known work environment to ground and frame theoretical principles.

Compassion fatigue and vicarious trauma

Asking workers to build relationships with troubled, traumatised, or addicted individuals, caught up in a cycle of complex and destructive behaviour, makes supervision a particularly important aspect of the psychologically

122 Staff support and training

informed care environment. To successfully support the client, the workers must feel confident that they too will be supported. Carers, by their nature, are susceptible to emotional contagion and countertransference, and without organised, supported time to reflect, may succumb to compassion fatigue.

Compassion fatigue is catastrophic for both worker and client. It can be defined as: 'a combination of physical, emotional, and spiritual depletion associated with caring for patients in significant emotional pain and physical distress',[10] and 'a state experienced by those helping people or animals in distress; it is an extreme state of tension and preoccupation with the suffering of those being helped to the degree that it can create a secondary traumatic stress for the helper'.[11]

Symptoms of compassion fatigue include:

- Avoidance of working with clients
- Emotional exhaustion, reduced empathy, and low patience
- More easily angry, irritable, cynical, or resentful
- Shifts in your ability to relate with compassion to clients or loved ones
- Hypochondria (fear of developing severe physical ailments)
- Hypervigilance (on guard, anxious, paranoid, irrational fears)
- Problems in personal relationships outside of work due to reduced compassion
- Doubting your competence/skill as a helper
- Feeling helpless towards clients
- Depression (feeling hopeless about yourself, clients, or the future)
- Suicidal thinking
- Diminished sense of satisfaction or enjoyment in your career
- Disruption of your worldview (e.g. difficulty trusting in people or viewing the world as unsafe as a result of hearing your clients' experiences of trauma)
- Intrusive imagery (often related to client stories)
- Hypersensitivity (or insensitivity or numbness) to emotionally charged material
- Loss or altered sense of self or reality[12]

Working in a PIE places an onus on workers to bear witness to the traumatised residents' stories. We know that sharing the traumatic experience with others is a precondition for the restitution of a sense of a meaningful world[13] and that supportive relationships are identified as an important aspect of trauma recovery.[14] As workers assist the resident to explore their histories, they too must be supported to protect themselves and avoid the damaging symptoms of compassion fatigue. Key to doing so is for supervisors to encourage conversation about experiencing any of these symptoms, and to create a culture where transparency and openness is encouraged and expected.

Vicarious trauma (VT) is another possibility which PIE workers, managers, and supervisors should remain consistently aware of. Outcomes of vicarious trauma are similar to those of compassion fatigue.

Here workers experience their own symptoms of trauma, resulting from being repeatedly exposed to other people's trauma and their stories of traumatic events. Inevitably a worker's worldview can be significantly changed as a result of bearing witness to these stories. Vicarious trauma is cumulative, building up over time, and the possibility of it affecting carers should be kept at the fore of managers' and supervisors' minds. Vicarious trauma is rife within frontline services – 39% of ambulance staff have experienced VT[15] and 40–80% of helping professionals experience high rates of secondary trauma.[16]

Symptoms of VT include:

- Social withdrawal
- Mood swings
- Aggression
- Greater sensitivity to violence
- Somatic symptoms
- Sleep difficulties
- Intrusive imagery
- Cynicism
- Sexual difficulties
- Difficulty managing boundaries with clients; and
- Problems with security, trust, esteem, intimacy, and control[17]

Supervision supports staff to become resilient, and to recognise that sharing stories and debriefing is a part of their own healing, and an integral part of their work. It has been documented that supportive supervision is a predictor of lower levels of vicarious trauma, working as a buffer against trauma reactions.[18] Recognising symptoms of vicarious trauma in workers is as important as it is to recognise trauma symptoms in clients to ensure their care giving and support is sustainable, after all: 'The expectation that we can be immersed in suffering and loss daily and not be touched by it is as unrealistic as expecting to be able to walk through water without getting wet.'[19]

In group supervision, team meetings, and individually, voicing emotional exhaustion and exploring personal experiences is a sign of strength and should be supported as such. Doing so gives team mates a chance to support and contextualise these feelings; and also to share their own struggles and successes that come with being in the caring role.

Whilst supervision is not a cure-all, it is recognised to be a main channel through which knowledge, values, and skills are transmitted; and as an emotionally safe space to examine and process key aspects of the care worker's experience.

This chapter has reflected KLOES:

S3

- 'The service is recognised as having an exceptional and inclusive approach to promoting the safety of its staff.'

E2

- 'Staff training is developed and delivered around individual needs.'

C1

- 'The service ensures staff that staff in all roles are highly motivated and offer care and support that is exceptionally compassionate and kind.'

W2

- 'Performance management processes are effective, reviewed regularly and reflect best practice.'

Notes

1 Sourced from www.bvs.co.uk/england-cqc-mandatory-training
2 www.cqc.org.uk/guidance-providers/regulations-enforcement/regulation-18-staffing
3 www.cqc.org.uk/what-we-do/how-we-do-our-job/fundamental-standards
4 Gladwell, M., *The Tipping Point* (Abacus, 2013), 12.
5 Cockersell, P. (Ed.), *Social Exclusion, Compound Trauma and Recovery* (Jessica Kingsley Publishers 2018), 101.
6 www.homeless.org.uk/sites/default/files/site-attachments/Creating%20a%20Psychologically%20Informed%20Environment%20-%202015.pdf, 9.
7 www.local.gov.uk/sites/default/files/documents/supervision-now-or-never-0a4.pdf
8 www.local.gov.uk/sites/default/files/documents/supervision-now-or-never-0a4.pdf

9 www.homeless.org.uk/sites/default/files/site-attachments/Creating%20a%20 Psychologically%20Informed%20Environment%20-%202015.pdf, 9.
10 Sourced from http://ojin.nursingworld.org/MainMenuCategories/ANAMarketplace/ANAPeriodicals/OJIN/TableofContents/Vol-16-2011/No1-Jan-2011/Compassion-Fatigue-A-Nurses-Primer.html
11 Sourced from www.compassionfatigue.org/
12 Sourced from https://healingrefuge.com/life-issues/compassion-fatigue-and-vicarious-trauma/
13 Herman, J., *Trauma and Recovery* (Basic Books, 1997), 70.
14 Evans, A. and Coccoma, P., *Trauma-Informed Care: How Neuroscience Influences Practice* (Routledge, 2014), 32.
15 Seen on BBC 1, Ambulance, 2019.
16 Sourced from https://vtt.ovc.ojp.gov/ojpasset/Documents/VT_Intro_To_VT_For_EMS-508.pdf
17 Sourced from https://en.wikipedia.org/wiki/Vicarious_traumatization#Signs_and_symptoms
18 Sourced from www.researchgate.net/profile/Roni_Berger/publication/270792673_Supervision_for_Trauma-Informed_Practice/links/552fc8470cf2f2a588a9c35c/Supervision-for-Trauma-Informed-Practice.pdf
19 Remen, N., 2006, sourced from https://addictionandrecoverynews.wordpress.com/tag/rachel-naomi-remen/

Conclusion

The shopkeeper

Becoming a PIE is like opening a shop, one in which we are selling care.

A shopkeeper makes their shop floor as conducive to sales as possible, they put great effort into window dressing and layout; into positioning their products to catch people's eye. If something isn't selling, they think of creative ways to advertise it, they alter the display.

A shopkeeper makes sure it is obvious his store is open – otherwise how can he lure in the buyers? He opens the door, puts displays out front, makes it colourful and welcoming. If there is no footfall he doesn't close up, but looks for innovative ways to attract shoppers. He might try opening earlier or later to catch early birds or stragglers, or try different offers.

Even when the shop is empty the owner is in there, waiting for a passing customer. After a long day they welcome customers with a smile, and are thankful for their purchase. The customer will not buy from a shopkeeper who is brusque, busy, or otherwise engaged.

There is no point in the shopkeeper going into the backroom to do the accounts if he hasn't sold anything. Repeatedly filling out columns will not make them turn from red to black – he has to be on the shop floor, gracious and welcoming, grateful for even the smallest sale – as they say, pennies make pounds.

It might be that a potential customer doesn't want to buy on that particular day. The shopkeeper still remains polite, knowing they might return later or tell a friend about the shop.

When sensing a sale, a skilled shopkeeper is on hand – neither pressurising nor distant – ready to catch the customer at just the right moment. Good service is skillful, recognised, and rewarded with a tip.

Finally, as a purchase is going through, the shopkeeper must be ready with change to honour their side of the transaction.

Working as a PIE means we must make the environment welcoming and considered, we should be creative in how we provide our care – and even when it feels we aren't getting anywhere, strive to remain open and accessible, ready and willing.

As residents purchase our care, using their experiences as currency, we must be wise enough to only ask for how much they can offer, ask too much and they will refuse to buy. We must be willing to give them change – some parts of our own experience.

Good shopkeepers open all day, every day, so customers become reliant on their convenience. So too should carers – providing consistency, reliability, and accessibility.

Shopkeepers are not paid per sale – but for all of their time in their shop, and are expected to use that time to improve sales. So too carers should move away from task-based achievement, and begin to look how their actions across a whole day can affect and improve the quality of their interactions – their 'sales'.

Keeping the books is a necessity, yet it doesn't help sales. Carers do not improve care by using repetitious paperwork and it stops them being available to the residents.

Balance

There is of course balance to be struck in the care environment between systemic obligation, legislation, and the individual. I hope that this book has gone some way to demonstrate that our systems can unintentionally harm the user, becoming an abrasive and coercive experience for them, especially those with complex needs, and that therefore we need to be consistently mindful of the interplay between user, environment, and worker. Using the PIE approach we can see how expectations placed upon the service – to provide a flow of information, for example, can harm the resident's development and autonomy. We have seen that we can be accidently retraumatising the very people we are trying to help, and have explored ways to creatively solve this issue.

Throughout this book I have argued that our system of 'streamlined' single-use services are creating inclusion criteria which, in effect, work as exclusion criteria for those most in need. The reliance on assessment, needed so that any duty team members can respond to a pool of clients, has led to an increasingly faceless system, confusing and threatening to the most vulnerable. Time and time again at Highwater House we have witnessed residents struggling to negotiate the bewildering number of different services and their varying protocols.

I have argued that the care home is an ideal supportive structure to help the resident access other helping services, and a space to gauge the *human* need, rather than being a reactive service moderating a specific set of symptoms or diagnosis, as others are. I have argued that use of multiple single-use services creates in people a fractured identity leading to professional patient-ism. A psychologically informed care environment, specifically focussed on Trauma-Informed Care, can be rehabilitative and healing.

Using the PIE approach helps us to recognise that the care home itself, and the support it offers, can also be a retraumatising experience for some. It can stir memories of childhood care, and be symbolic of shame as people struggle to accept help. After spending a lifetime ricocheting between both needing and rejecting the system, the care home, used well, can be a placatory and cathartic environment.

Recovery

'The course of recovery does not follow a simple progression', writes Herman, 'but often detours and doubles back'.[1] Recovery, then, is not linear. Just as everybody in the community has good and bad days, ebbs and flows of mood and substance or alcohol use, phases of happiness and mental unrest, we have seen that residents should be allowed the freedom to do so as well; their human experience welcomed and celebrated. In the psychologically informed care home we recognise the causes of, and therefore support, the erratic and self-damaging behaviour of our residents believing that given the right environment and time, people will err towards homeostasis and self-actualisation.

You cannot medicate memories, and memories affect behaviour: we can however provide a thoughtful, considerate environment where new, less painful memories can be created; these too then will affect behaviour, but positively. We can be the group that bears witness to stories of trauma, aiding the process of recovery; a journey of discovery.

Interdependence not independence

Humans are social creatures. We rely on our peers to help us moderate our behaviour, and emotional connection to guide our actions. Independence can too often mean isolation, and the incessant drive of recovery services to 'promote independence' can be damaging to the survivor who is slowly healing their trauma, using the group dynamic to learn, or relearn, how to successfully relate to the world. Skillful, psychologically informed workers can help the resident negotiate this emotionally fraught path without them becoming de-skilled or helpless. Healing trauma – rejecting the short-termism of substance use, or changing self-destructive but safe-making behaviour – is akin to taking off a useful but damaged coat and leaving oneself vulnerable to the elements, before finding and pulling on a new, more suitable one. This process will take people different amounts of time – and we, the PIE workers, who have asked them to take off that old coat, must adapt to *their* growth at *their* pace, not ours – otherwise we risk sending people out, uncoated, into the cold.

The reliance the resident feels upon the workers and the care home is natural as they form new secure attachments, the dependability a novel and exciting prospect. Given time, and as part of their healing process, they will know when they are ready to move on. The skilled worker recognises when it is time to support this next step, when it is time for the resident to explore elsewhere.

This interdependence – the resident able to trust the workers and the service, the workers confident in their connection – means the resident can leave the service as an equal; on their terms.

To conclude

To work in a PIE is, in essence, to ask 'why?' Why is the resident behaving like that? What are the causes?

By asking this, we open ourselves and the resident to a shared narrative of exploration, change and hope.

In many ways the answer too is quite simple.

> 'Three things in human life are important: the first is to be kind; the second is to be kind; and the third is to be kind.'[2]

Using the PIE principles, ultimately, helps workers to be kind.

Notes

1 Herman, J., *Trauma and Recovery* (Basic Books, 1997), 213.
2 Quote from Henry James.

Index

3 Rs 13–14, 105–106, 112; *see also* responsiveness; roles; rules

abandonment 50, 62; expectation of 66; fear of 33, 61, 66, 70; feelings of 56
abuse 12, 18–23, 26, 28–29, 31, 33, 37, 53, 56, 64, 80, 88–89, 93, 108; institutional 56; mental 56; physical 60; psychological 56; *see also* childhood abuse; sexual abuse; substance abuse/misuse
acceptance 3, 29, 36, 39, 42, 76, 93, 101, 106–107
addiction 3, 6, 9, 27, 36, 38, 40, 46, 50, 77, 81, 85, 91, 93, 107, 118; alcohol 37; chronic 9; cycle 38; *see also* substance abuse/misuse
Adverse Childhood Experience (ACE) questionnaire 17, 21–22
agency 52, 89; self- 43, 71
aggression 28, 32, 46, 50–52, 56–59, 61–62, 69–71, 123
amygdala 31
anger 20, 23, 33, 35, 49–50, 57, 68–69, 80
anxiety 9, 12, 18, 20, 28–29, 32, 38, 50, 60, 71, 77, 89–94, 103; chronic 9, 38; *see also* social anxiety
Asperger's 77
attachment 20, 32, 81, 129
attachment theory 35, 61, 66, 79, 121
auditing 4, 15, 97, 117
autonomy 23, 43, 63, 71, 91, 127

Banduras 71
Beck, Aaron 69

behaviour management 55, 57, 112; techniques 2
behaviours: acceptable 29, 62; aggressive 50, 59–60, 62; anti-social 5, 28–29, 34, 36, 55, 57, 62, 64–65, 70–71; bad 62; challenging 3, 10, 46, 51–52, 56, 72, 76, 78, 90, 94, 115; complex 3, 46, 76; dangerous 70, 77, 81; defiant 70; demanding 21, 70; difficult 55, 58, 61, 69–70; disruptive 62; erratic 77, 101; extreme 29, 43; as form of communication 26; harmful 9; healthy 43; negative 60, 66; positive 66, 71; prosocial 64–65, 106; risky 58; self-defeating 27, 32, 76; self-destructive 33, 50, 53, 58, 61, 77; survivor 58; visible 69; volatile 70; *see also* behaviour management
bias 8, 20, 46, 52, 58, 70, 80, 84–85, 98; and roles 52–53
borderline personality disorder 12
boundaries 6, 20–21, 29, 31, 34, 43, 47, 51, 55–57, 59–62, 64–65, 67–72, 87, 106, 118–119, 123; elastic/flexible 56, 65; safe 47, 55; *see also* social boundaries
brain development 3
Britain 111; *see also* UK, the
burnout 77, 79; *see also* compassion fatigue

Care Act 56, 70, 85
care environment 9, 31, 39, 42, 48, 53, 69, 79, 84, 92, 122, 127–128;

Index 131

see also Psychologically Informed Environment (PIE)
care homes 2, 13, 43, 84, 88, 91, 117; PIE 2, 13, 40–41, 43, 47, 80, 108–109, 111; reflective practice in 47, 53; registered 6, 75, 114, 119; residential 1–2, 4, 5–6, 8, 84, 97
Care Quality Commission (CQC) 1–2, 4, 26, 56, 89, 97, 115, 117; inspection 1–2; Key Lines of Enquiry (KLOES) 2, 15, 26, 73, 82, 95, 103, 105, 113, 124
carers 7–10, 20, 22, 24, 29, 31, 34, 36, 40, 43, 56, 64, 69, 75–76, 78, 81, 88, 105, 112, 114, 116, 118, 122–123, 127
childhood abuse 9, 19–20, 22, 36, 88
children's home 12, 22
chronic disease 21
clients: complex 3; hard-to-reach 42; marginalised 26; problem 65; traumatised 35, 57, 110; unmanageable 27; unreachable 9, 27, 112; vulnerable 52, 107; *see also* residents; revolving door clients/patients
cognitive behavioural therapy (CBT) 14, 69, 78–79
collective efficacy 23
communal space 86–87
community 3, 5, 10, 19, 21, 42, 48, 53, 56, 61, 66, 79, 84, 92–93, 101, 106–107, 128
co-morbidity 5
compassion fatigue 34–35, 50, 60, 76, 79, 114, 121–123; definition 122; symptoms of 122; *see also* vicarious trauma
complex needs 1–3, 5, 7, 9, 12, 46, 53, 80, 91, 106, 117, 127
conflict management 6
congruence 33, 49
connectedness 23
coping mechanisms 29
counselling 9, 36, 43, 70, 118
countertransference 27, 122
counterwill 63, 87, 103
crack 20, 38
Creating a Psychologically Informed Environment 87–88, 100, 116–117
crisis intervention 19
cycle of change 78–79, 111

de-escalation, principle of 57
defence mechanism 32, 61; *see also* self-defence mechanism
depression 21, 81, 122
detachment 28
Dialectical Behavioural Therapy (DBT) 78, 116
Dickens, Charles 55
disconnection 22–23
discrimination 52, 82
disempowerment 22–23
dislocation 18
drug and alcohol services 9, 97
dual diagnosis 2, 5–6, 9; definition 5

elastic tolerance 2, 55–73, 87
emergency services 2, 100–101
'emotional algebra' 30–32
emotional contagion 71, 122
emotional literacy 32, 79, 107, 114
empathy 10, 14, 33–34, 44, 57, 73, 75, 79, 81–82, 107, 109, 113, 116, 122
empowerment 23, 106, 109, 112
Enabling Environment standards 13
eviction 50, 65–66, 70, 100
evidence 13–15, 97–103, 105
evidence gathering/evidencing 15, 97
exclusion 65–66, 90, 127; *see also* social exclusion

food 29, 47, 67–68, 93–94, 108, 114
friendship 7, 31, 35, 38, 108
frontline services 9, 123
frontline staff 36, 116

Ghandi, Mahatma 107
Gibbs 46, 48; *see also* reflective cycle
Gladwell, M. 115; *see also* tipping point
group dynamics 49, 53, 71, 99, 128
group work 9, 11, 118
guilt 33

hallucinations 18
Health and Social Care Act 89, 115, 117
health and social care industry 2
helplessness 19–20, 22, 31, 33, 93, 106
Herman, Judith 10, 18, 20, 23, 31, 93, 110, 128

heroin 12, 20–21, 38–39, 52, 68, 76–77, 101–102
Highwater House 1–3, 5–6, 9, 15, 19, 22–23, 26, 28, 36, 51–52, 59, 63, 65, 67–68, 78–79, 85–86, 88–89, 91–94, 99–101, 106–108, 110–112, 115–116, 118, 127
homelessness 5–6, 20
homeless people 1, 5, 27, 79
homeostasis 28, 56, 80, 128
hope 3, 23, 27–28, 32–33, 35, 53, 76, 81, 93, 99–100, 113, 129
hopelessness 22, 35, 58, 81, 122
hyperarousal 32, 77
hypervigilance 20, 58, 69, 71, 122

incarceration 22
inclusion 66, 90, 103; criteria 9, 36, 58, 127; narrative of 66
inclusivity 106–108
interdependence 128–129
isolation 3, 6, 18–20, 23, 27, 46, 51, 56, 58, 64, 70, 72, 91, 128

Key Lines of Enquiry *see* Care Quality Commission (CQC)
kindness 10, 24, 59, 61, 75, 78–79, 81, 94, 107–109, 115

language 14, 17, 32, 35, 48, 58, 62, 64, 66, 72, 99, 105–108, 110, 113, 115, 121; clinical 42–43; common/shared 40–43, 110; emotional 35, 79, 109; and relationship building 26; of recovery 41, 43; technical 43; therapeutic 121; of trauma 58, 72
learning difficulties 12
Levy, J. 42

malignant social psychology 105–106
mealtimes 68, 84, 94
medication: anti-psychotic 18, 40, 51
mental health 1, 5, 7, 9, 19–20, 22, 26, 39, 41–42, 71, 100–101, 112; *see also* mental health services; mental health system; mental health wards
Mental Health Act 9, 23, 101, 109
Mental Health Recovery Star 97, 100

mental health services 9, 18, 80, 97, 101, 118
mental health system 10, 17, 36, 53, 67, 81, 93, 111, 115
mental health wards 19, 64, 68, 77, 85, 91, 110
mental ill-health 6, 27, 85, 93, 98
mental illness 3, 12, 19, 76, 81, 99; *see also* mental ill-health
mentalization 79
methadone 11, 37, 101
mistrust 12, 18, 22, 28, 31–32, 34, 38, 41, 58, 68–69, 89, 93–94
morphine 101
motivational interviewing 78–79

narrative 3, 56, 62, 66, 80, 86–87, 94, 110, 116; of acceptance 76, 101; arc 93; collective 112; of inclusion and success 66; personal 10, 111; public 112–113; of safety 68; strengths-based 42; *see also* narrative therapy; narrative work
narrative therapy 42, 79–80, 99; approach 99
narrative work 97, 99
National Council for Behavioural Health 109
National Specifications 91
negative projection 33
NHS 51
NICE guidelines 57
night shelter 5–6
No-one Left Out Solutions Ltd 87
'normality' 19
nutrition 93–94

operant conditioning 79
opiates 77

'parachute period' 111
paranoia 18, 23, 46, 68, 80, 87, 90, 94
paranoid schizophrenia 12, 77, 102
patients 55, 81, 111, 122; *see also* professional patients; residents; revolving door clients/patients
patterning 71
persecution, feelings of 39, 90
perseverance 75

Index

personality disorder 5; *see also* borderline personality disorder
person-centred approach/care/culture/work 1–2, 26, 33, 41, 44, 54, 82, 85, 95, 103, 106, 112–113
positive reinforcement 57
power dynamics 103, 121
power equity 53
power imbalance 22, 31, 33, 36, 39, 53, 69, 81, 86, 88
powerlessness 80, 85, 103
pre-treatment pathways 42, 79
professional bias 80, 98
professionalism 34–35, 38, 109
professional patients 35, 38, 41–43, 65, 98, 118; -ism 80, 128
projective identification 33
proportionality, principle of 56, 70, 91
pro-social modelling 79
protection, principle of 56
psychiatric medical model 18
psychological awareness 13–15, 28, 57, 75–82, 107, 110, 115–116
psychologically informed approach 21, 94
Psychologically Informed Environment (PIE) 1, 6, 26, 87; approach 1, 3, 26–27, 35, 42, 46, 66, 87–88, 100, 106, 110, 114, 116, 127–128; care homes 2, 13, 40–41, 43, 47, 80, 108–109, 111; concept 42; definition 8–10; ethos 115, 120; formula 3; framework 1–2, 7–8, 10, 26, 33, 36, 57, 60, 78, 117; ideology 42; initiative 13, 46, 115, 118; interview 109; language 115; pre- 87; staff 24; training 114; workers 23, 28, 30–31, 33–36, 38, 53, 58, 60–61, 69, 71, 93, 98, 102–103, 123, 129; *see also* Psychologically Informed Environment (PIE) model; Psychologically Informed Environment (PIE) principles
Psychologically Informed Environment (PIE) model 1, 7–8, 13, 15, 22, 116, 119; Residential (PIE-R) 15, 75
Psychologically Informed Environment (PIE) principles 1–4, 7, 9, 13, 23, 38, 53, 66, 88, 90–92, 100–101, 105, 109–110, 112–113, 114–115, 119, 121, 129; PIE 2.0 13–14, 78, 105; *see also* care environment; evidence gathering/evidencing; psychological awareness; Psychologically Informed Environment (PIE) model; reflective practice; relationships; residents; responsiveness; roles; rules; spaces of opportunity; staff support; staff training
Psychologically Informed Services for Homeless People – Good Practice Guide 8
psychological projection 61
psychosis 18, 68, 77, 101
psychotic break 18
psychotic episodes 12, 21
PTSD 12
punitive measures 56–57, 60, 62, 68, 70

reciprocal determinism 79, 121
recovery 10–11, 23–24, 27, 42–43, 56, 81, 106, 108, 128; cycle 107; language of 41, 43; process 53, 71, 86; stages of 10; trauma 9, 32, 106–107, 111–112, 122
recovery model 19
recruitment process 105, 109
reflective cycle 46, 48–50
reflective practice 7, 13, 15, 26, 46–54, 56, 117–118; definition 47–48
relationship building 7–8, 13, 24, 26, 32–35, 38, 40, 43, 46–47, 58, 86, 89, 93–94, 102, 121; and language 26
relationship equation 30
relationships 1, 7–8, 10, 13, 15, 21–24, 26–44, 47, 49, 56, 64, 67, 71, 81, 93, 97, 100, 108–109, 117; and addiction 38–40; forging 27–28; 'helping' 33; impersonal 76; negative 30, 32; peer 31; personal 122; positive 26, 30–32, 34, 44; among residents 71–72, 102; staff 95; staff and resident 1, 26–28, 35, 41, 49, 52, 55, 63–65, 85–90, 93–94, 102, 105–106, 108–109, 116–117; trauma and 31–32; trusting 1, 7, 13, 31, 44, 47, 49, 57, 69, 86, 93, 102, 109; *see also* relationship building; relationship equation

Index

residential care home 1–2, 4, 5–6, 8, 84, 97
residential care service users *see* residents
residents: and addiction 50, 118; behaviours of 9, 32–34, 53, 61, 63, 67, 75, 128; care of 35, 79, 112, 127; challenging 2, 6, 66; choices of 33, 72, 89, 106; drug misuse of 40; dually diagnosed 36; experiences/life stories of 3, 22–23, 31, 43, 47, 85, 88, 103, 110, 112; and food 93–94; growth of 99–100; needs of 2, 6, 9, 24, 88–89; relationships with other residents 71–72, 102; relationships with staff 1, 26–28, 35, 41, 49, 52, 55, 63–65, 85–90, 93–94, 102, 105–106, 108–109, 116–117; strengths of 3; and transition 111–112; traumatised 24, 84, 88, 122; wellbeing of 58, 86–87, 91; *see also* professional patients; revolving door clients/patients
resilience 22, 27, 32, 34, 38, 75–77, 109, 123
responsiveness 13, 15, 31, 47, 75, 105, 110–111
retraumatisation 67, 69, 72, 84, 89, 99, 110, 127–128
revictimization 67, 81, 93
revolving door clients/patients 12, 18, 41, 56, 58, 76
risk assessment 18, 36, 41, 58, 60, 70, 98
risk management 73
Rogers, Carl 13, 27, 32–34, 76, 80, 98
roles 7, 13, 15, 22, 35, 52, 63, 70, 75, 81, 86, 93, 102, 105, 108–109, 111, 118, 124
rules 13, 15, 31, 55–57, 62–67, 70, 75, 87, 93, 98, 105–108; vs. boundaries 64–65

safety 7–8, 18, 23, 27, 35, 37, 43, 59, 63, 68, 73, 85, 87–88, 91–92, 103, 106, 114–115, 118, 124; emotional 87, 115; psychological 115
sanctions 64, 70
schizophrenia 39; *see also* paranoid schizophrenia

secondary trauma 122–123; *see also* vicarious trauma
sectioning 9, 12, 18, 21, 77, 85
security 31, 35, 60, 68, 70, 116, 123; in- 19
self-actualisation 86, 128
self-care 77, 81, 100
self-defence mechanism 61
self-efficacy 19, 23
self-esteem 33, 42, 81, 100
Self-Medication Hypothesis 40, 77–79
service users 1, 4, 7–8, 12, 31, 51–53, 55–58, 71, 85, 88–89, 98, 108, 110–111; chronic 41; long-term 42; transient 18; *see also* resident
sexual abuse 12, 20, 37, 60
shame 20, 22–23, 33, 36–37, 40, 53, 65–66, 68–69, 128
shared values 65, 107–108
sobriety 36, 60, 80
social anxiety 9
social boundaries 57, 64
social exclusion 1, 26
social learning theory 71
social services 18, 41–42
spaces of opportunity 13–14
staff morale 1, 27, 109, 117
staff supervision 36, 46, 57, 65, 94, 114–124; open-door policy 117–118
staff support 13, 15, 75, 114–124
staff support and training 15, 75, 114–124
staff training 13, 15, 24, 35, 53–54, 75, 78–79, 82, 94, 100, 109, 114–124
stigmatisation 5, 52, 58; de- 10
St Martins 5–6, 100, 107, 110; House 5–6
street drinker 48, 59
structural violence 85, 99, 110, 121
substance abuse/misuse 5, 12, 76, 78; services 80
suicide 12, 21–22
survivors 12, 18–21, 23, 28, 31, 33, 36, 46, 58, 61, 67, 81, 88, 93, 106, 111, 115, 128

therapeutic communities 10, 56
therapy 36; person-centred 33; psychological 13; solution-focussed 100; talking 114; *see also* cognitive behavioural therapy; narrative

Index

therapy; Trauma-Informed Care and Dialectical Behavioural Therapy (DBT)
time-outs 2, 65–66, 68–70, 88, 101; graded 65
tipping point 79, 87, 115
transference 27, 34; *see also* countertransference
trauma 17–24, 27, 30–31, 33–36, 43, 53, 57–58, 60, 69, 77, 81, 94, 110–111, 121–123; from abuse 9, 18; childhood 3, 9, 20–22, 31, 93; chronic 20; complex 20; compound 7, 20–21, 24; from domestic violence 18; language of 58, 72; psychological 18, 23, 71; recovery from 9, 32, 106–107, 111–112, 122; and relationships 31–32; survivors 18–19, 36, 46, 61, 67, 81, 93, 106, 111, 115; type I 19–20; type II 19–20; from war 18; *see also* PTSD; secondary trauma; trauma-informed care/practice (TIC); vicarious trauma
Trauma-Informed Care and Dialectical Behavioural Therapy (DBT) 78, 116
trauma-informed care/practice (TIC) 1, 10, 17–24, 27, 56, 78–79, 81, 105, 109–110, 116–117, 120, 128
tri-morbidity 20, 80, 91

UK 19, 78
unconditional positive regard 33–34, 39
Under-1-Roof 100–101
untoward incidents 1–2, 66, 88, 101

vicarious trauma (VT) 35–38, 79, 114, 121–124

wet environment 63
workers 92–93; care 1, 94, 106, 116, 118; domestic 94, 115; frontline 2; health 102; in-house 42; as mediators 72; non-clinical 80; PIE 23, 28, 30–31, 33–36, 38, 53, 58, 60–61, 69, 71, 93, 98, 102–103, 123, 129; role of 72; as rule-makers 63, 72, 108; support services 10; *see also* carers; staff morale; staff supervision; staff support; staff support and training; staff training

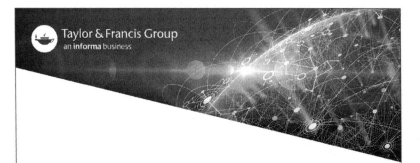